A
Global
Nation

Book One

By Dan Mason

ISBN 978-1-4303-1793-7
BCID # 788-4259606

Dedication

I dedicate this book to my Lord and Savior Jesus Christ, without whom, this book would not be possible. I thank my Lord and my God for all the truth and revelations that He has given me and led me to my walk with Him.

I have been in the process of writing a book since early 1990. This book speaks for my views on Christ and the coming world government.

Content

Preface

The Narrator of our story is Juan "Carlos" Gardner. Juan is the main character in my first Novel- "The Fading Republic" due out in 2007. In A Global Nation, Juan outlines for us the decline and destruction of the United States through cause and effect.

He is the Narrator that will guide us through the maze of lies and disinformation. It is through his eyes that we are brought face to face with the truth concerning the Global Conspiracy.

Introduction

Our journey to a New Home

"Vanity of vanities, saith the Preacher, vanity of vanities; all is vanity."
ECCLESIASTES 1:2

A Global Nation is Mankind's final frontier. It is his destination; it is the end of his journey, his new home. On the spaceship called Earth, the Global Elites are in the driver's seat. They are headed for the union of differing worlds. A union of nations. Their swain song is the call for an era of peace, harmony, justice and prosperity for all.

"There should, however, be no illusion that a global police force run by a global democracy is feasible. Those who have carried the winning ideas to the top of the mountain, and now wish to spread them, will not allow this process to be vetoed by the semi-converted or by plain toughs...

And if that sounds painless, it is not. The mountaintop is thick with those who would rather not see trade that is liberal, aid that is too principled, or arms control that is too self-denying. And America needs to remember that a willingness to involve others is not enough to make a collective world order work. There must also be readiness to submit to it. If America really wants such an order, it will have to be ready to take its complaints to the GATT, finance the multilateral aid agencies, submit itself to the International Court, bow to some system to monitor arms export, and make a habit of consulting the U.N."
The Economist-June 28, 1991

It's a Small World

We are more in touch with other people the world over now that technology has brought us together and as earth's population has increased. Now because of the threat of nuclear war and between and nuclear terrorism, many in the world are searching for peace and stability.

The world in the past has looked to America to establish peace on earth. But the American World Order has not provided peace for the world. So the world is looking to another Order for this peace.

The Globalist and the genetically superior have the answers for us all, men like Noble Prize winner James D. Watson will unveil to us their plan for a better world.

In this new global system, there will be a new economic, social and religious Order for the people of earth. The Globalist promise us a dawning of a new day. This Global Nation they promise is just in time for the world's third millennium since the birth of Christ.

Many believe that Mother Earth, through nature, is preparing herself for the coming future events. We can see the step taken by the Globalist as it develops the world into regional powers to resist the Christian World Order. And to prepare itself for the day when the America World Order will collapse. The hunt for a better Pagan Order is on.

In A Global Nation, we will find out what kind of a Union or Global Order is on the minds of the World Leaders. We will see that it is a Global Government, a Universal Order. As the Globalist and their supporters bombarded us daily with their dream of hope to Mankind. We see more and more join the choir and sang the praise for the coming Utopia. This dream has been their goal, and they know that they need to form a Global Union of Nations to control all living creature, they will not to achieve their goal without it.

INTRODUCTION

Through fear of terrorism and an escalation of the war in Iraq, they have the world's attention! With the threaten War in Iran and Korea, there is an increase in tensions the world over. Mankind has begun to cries out for a different World Order, and seeks a different way to achieve its dream other than the America Way. Mankind seeks a way to bring about an everlasting world peace.

The people of earth and their world leaders are looking far and wide to find this great hope, they are looking for a Savoir. A strong man to grab hold of the rings of power and become the master of the ship of state. The world has been on this journey for world peace for sometime now; it has been a long and bloody journey. They want to pull into port and rest.

Many have lost hope in our world system; no longer do we look favorably at the Nations-States system. Mankind is weighting its other options for a world of tomorrow, a world not yet charted. Mankind is looking to form a Global Nation. But one most ask the question, will this achieve a more Perfect Global Union? Will this bring us our long awaited rest and world peace?

So my friend, the stage is set, and the curtain is falling on the Nation-State stage and is rising on the Universal Nation's one. I truly believe in the not to distance future a New World Order will arise, and in this Order, I believe that the Nation-States will be compelled to surrender their sovereignty for the greater good of humanity. And I believe that America will be the force and the enforcer for this movement? Their war cry has gone out-It is join us or die! America has started the process with the Democratization of the world.

At first glance, this may seem to be a good thing for the world. Here we have America standing up to the world leaders and saying to them, "You will answer to your people, you will give your people a voice.

And to the people of the world America says, "You will be free and you will have your say in the government that rules you." But truly why has America taken on this role? Why are we forcing others to bow down to our way of life?

American World Empire

As we look at the process of a maturing and a declining democracy over time, we can see the growth of corruption in the local and national leaders and in the people themselves, until the democracy becomes a welfare and a police state.

As you read A Global Nation. I hope you will find some answers to your many questions in life. I hope to uncover for you the steps that we have taken on this journey to our new home.

I hope you will see in these pages the mystery behind the new world order. I hope you will see the hand of the Puppet Master redirecting our future, our cosmos. And bring our world into a new age before our very own eyes.

Now let us ask our future masters some questions. In this New World Order...

1. Will this monster of a government become the master of the people, or will the people master it? Will this government really do for us and for the rest of Mankind all that it says it will do?
2. In this new global system of world government. Will it truly be for the betterment of all Mankind?
3. In this coming world police state and welfare state. Will it make the world a much happier and safer place to live? Or will it just make us wards and slaves to the state.

Many Americans wish to see a Global Country born within this century. They seek a Global Nation, that is, they seek a Global Government. To accomplish this, they plan on creating a new civil rights movement. To do this, they are preaching and proclaiming to the people that they have a new human right, the right to have a world community.

The Third America Revolution

Those that seek this New World Order claim that they seek a peaceful revolution, but nonetheless, they seek a revolution. They to seek to empower the voters, the people of the world, to compel their politicians, their national leaders, to commit each of their individual nations, to implement these global solutions that they will outline for us.

As we look around the world today, everyone seems to be in search of the perfect place to live, the perfect world. Mankind in time past has tried to make heaven on earth; there was Nineveh, Babylon, Egypt, Athens and Rome. Mankind has sought peace in Africa, in Europe, in America. So you can see that this dream is an Old Idea, which has a new beginning in our world today. It is Eden reborn.

Some call it Utopia, some call it Heaven, and still others call it Paradise. Some are seeking it through Communism, Racism, Socialism, Religion, and Capitalism. Just to name a few.

But if we were to take a closer look around the world today, we would see that most people, tongues and nations are in the dismantling and destroying mode, and not the rebuilding mode.

The Globalist are no different, they feel that they must clear off the Old World Orders and bring in the New. Therefore, this New World Order will effect and impact your life. In this coming world order, you must choose which side you are on. You must choose whose slave you will be.

They are reshaping the world today into the image that they wish it to be. It is an image that they have created, it is their vision. Not all of us will be able to fit into this image.

They are more than willing to use any means available to them to acquire this New Home. And in doing so, they know that they will have to kill off millions of us, if not billions of us, that are in their way. Yes, we are in their way, they feel we are holding up their progress. Therefore we have to go and our God with us.

They do not understand that they will never get to there holy land, this new world from here. They will never reach their goal. For it is the self that they wish to glorify. And if they were to reach their goal, would be as short lived as Hitler's dream world was.

They will try and create their perfect world on the backs and broken bodies of others. In these groups, we see that it is by their own will and their own achievements and their own hard work which they seek to accomplish this New Order. They have no need of God or for you.

Mission Statement

They have lied and they will lie again to create their heaven on earth. The end justifies the means. They will do what is necessary to reach their goal. They have told the world that they are seeking peace. But what they are seeking is peace without you. For they are seeking a world that conforms to their will.

There is no end to their resources and their avenues to reaching their new home. In a Global Nation, we will take a journey on a road to discovery. You will be amazed at what you will find.

Helpers and Supporters

They have many working in the shadows and on the back stages for the New World Order. Some are visible and an others are invisible. And then there are the Puppet Masters.

I do not have all the answers. But in a Global Nation, we will look at the groups and their supporters. We will look at the goals of the Global agenda. We will look at the members of the

CFR and the Skull and Bones. Then we will uncover their actions and their beliefs in the coming pages.

We will look to those that have gone before us, those that have tried to expose the tactics of the players and their groups to the world. They have tried to show us the hidden agendas and plans of these men of renown.

Men like Alex Jones, A. Ralph Epperson, Malachi Martin, Carroll Quigley, Chalmers Johnson, and Lou Dobbs. They have been at work exposing the lies and the liars.

Many of them have been attacked for their stance and their beliefs. Some because they have taken on the secret government. For that they have been labeled villains and traitors by those that have sold out their country. This is all done because the Globalist intend to enslave the world.

As you search for answers, please hear them out. Do not allow the enemy of the people to gain your trust. The traitors will try and destroy their names. You must look around the smoke screens that they have put up to hide their evil activities. Here we will look into their motives and their agendas. Now let us begin.

One

The Mob

"If freedom of speech is taken away, then dumb and silent we may be led, like sheep to the slaughter."
George Washington

For the most part, the people of the world are just uninitiated spectators on the sidelines of life. They have no idea how the process of government or governing takes place, and they could care less about what is going on inside the halls of justice until it involves them.

They are blind to their leader's beliefs and the political actions taken on the orders of the mighty lobbyists. They have no concern about the hurt and harm being done to them by the European trained politicians with a worldview. To hear the common citizen tell it, all is right with the world. Just keep the beer, sex, drugs and Rock and Roll coming, and all will be eternally happy.

I know the feeling. I have been their myself. To think otherwise would bring a man face to face with his greatest fears. Most men do not serve God on a daily bases. The need for God only comes at holidays, baptisms, funerals, and the occasional tragedy.

So therefore, most men only speak to God just before or after a great tragedy in the world or in his personal life. So they must think only of the good times, less they feel guilty in their hearts. Men seek after fun to cover the despair in their morbid lives. For this world is their only home. This is all they will ever have. This book is geared toward them. Those that are in the fog and the haze of life. It is my hope that some of them can be delivered from the fire to come, here on earth and in hell.

At least if they take the time to read this book, they will be made aware of the coming World Economy, the Global Government and the One World State Religion. God first sends a warning before He sends the Judgment.

Hear and Believe

Most people still laugh when I try and tell them of the coming police state, one world government, the illuminati and the coming world enslavement. But I continue, for the people must be told, they must hear the truth.

There are many writers and personalities in the Conspiracy Theory camp and the Patriot Movement who still believe that by informing the people, one day the people will have enough information and that the people will then rise up and overthrow the government.

I personally feel that they are naïve and misled. This is clearly not my aim here. Then there are those that do not want any form of government at all or of any kind and they would lead this world into chaos. I feel that they are very dangerous and self destructive, they are the anarchist in the world.

I believe that the end is near for the world and that God will not reverse this course and this action. It may or may not be delayed, but it will not reverse.

For God has called down Judgment upon America and it is coming, and it is coming very soon. Our only hope and our only safety is in Christ Jesus. You will not find safety in man or his government. Many will fight on believing that they have a chance to make a difference, as did the Zealots in the days of Christ, but they well fight in vain and so will you.

From me to You

This is a work from my heart as much as from my head. I can see that the people are perishing without the truth. That they are worshiping at the altar of the Television. Therefore, they cannot see the coming danger. For they receive their only knowledge from the is. This evil one-eyed monster is their teacher and their preacher.

The television is geared to draw out our lusts and weaknesses and not our strengths. It is a tool used well by the Masters of the Universe. We feed from it daily.

Your house and your family would be better off without it. That would make a big difference in your life if you could learn to live without it. But you will not. It is your babysitter, your child raiser and your schoolteacher. It commands the center of your life and your home. That places "them" in the center of your lives and your home also.

Why have we fallen?

America is blinded. As the North America Trade Union takes shape right before our eyes. Many Americans do not believe what they are seeing. As Canada, America and Mexico are dropping their borders, they are interchanging their Social Security policies. They will have no need for border enforcement. Each country is integrating country. This is happening as America and its values decline.

Americans are blind to this integration and the cause of this decline in America's value system. Most America do not have any idea of what is going on in their own country. It is not the immigrates but the Americans that have lowered their values and standards. So when immigrates arrive in America, they are not faced with a higher moral standard but with a lower one.

This is the house that we have built. This is the country and the society that we love and cherish. America fells to see our country is a Broke Back and backslidden society. The reason that America can not recognize its problems, is because, this is the society of our own choosing. We have gotten here because we are a backslidden nation, and have been from the start. But not in the areas that plague us now.

Race

Our nation did not face the race issue head on. So the Race issue became a serpent's egg among the blessing of this nation. Those eggs hatched in the 1800s, and the war is not over yet.

This fighting will go on into World War Three. There will never be a true peace among the races. There has never been true peace upon the earth, not since Adam and Eve first fell to temptation.

There will always be tension. It is human nature. Just as there is tension between a man and his wife. There will be tension among us. But tension is sometimes good.

Tension is what holds a tire on the road while you drive. The tension from the outside and from within should have drawn us together.

But the sin of racism has cost us much more than slavery ever gave this nation. As we see with the Hebrews in Egypt. Slavery will lead a nation down a dead-end path.

For slavery was as much a moral decay for the white man as it was for the black. We are still paying for it and we will pay for it until the end of our days.

Death by neglect

There are those who clearly see the sins of this nation and its slide into corruption. As a nation, we are all guilty. In this book, I will speak of the elite and their push for the One World Government. But to speak of that and their sins and overlook our own sins would be foolish.

Our sins brought us here and that has given them their power over us. It is our neglect of the Lord's work that has allowed the devil to carry on with his own work. This is a judgment from God. Our only escape is in Christ Jesus.

Demi-Gods

This idea of a World Order is an old idea with a new face. And because we live in a world filled with transgression, and because we all suffer from a sinful nature, we cannot see the spiritual death of this nation with our natural eyes. It truly takes the hand of God to lead us out from under this darkness and out of this sin.

We hate, and we are hated. We envy, and we are envied, we deceive, and we are deceived. And still we get nowhere. Christ is our only hope.

To the Christian I say, we know we need to go to church, but we do not. To all mankind I say, Christ is our only hope, Christ is our only choice.

As a people, we sin and we have deceived ourselves into believing that it is all right. We decide to live like animals and try and justify it by saying, 'Well I am just not religious.'

That only shows that we fail to see that Christ did not call us to be religious, he called us to love Him and keep His Commandments. And they are Commandments; they are not Options or Opinions. When we keep these teachings, we will not be religious, we will be God-fearing Christians. We will have a fellowship with Christ.

Hide a lie within the Truth

Now as the Serpent was in the Garden of Eden with Eve, and his Seed with us. You must understand. They do tell us some of the truth, but even that is shaded in some way.

On first look, we may think that we understood what they meant, but we really do not, for we do not have the key or the code to decipher their message, therefore we cannot understand, we only thought we understood, understand? Sic!

That way, they make the people feel that they belong. They are a part of and take part in the knowledge. They belong to the in crowd, the people struggle to understand, but who wants to be the first person to ask the first and most obvious question? It will only make you look stupid, so we all play along as if we know what they are all talking about.

For the masses or the mob, they could care less, but they have to put on a show, less someone would be the wiser for it. They are more than aware that the truth is too much for the average person to handle, and that it truly is too hard to hide. So, therefore, they plant among it the serpent's seed, the lie. They must ensure that there is enough smoke to cover their actions and their deeds to the very end.

That is why they have to breed hate. Therefore, the new world order becomes a Jewish Conspiracy and not a global one. It becomes a Zionist Movement and not a devilish one. In that way, we all fail to see the black man, the white man, the brown man and the yellow man among the conspirators. This has been the problem from the beginning for so many people.

Look at the Tower of Babel; we all were there, in one city, under one government, following one false religion. Now that religion has moved to Rome. This is beyond the races. This is a global evil that spans every race and we all played or still play a part in it. One way or other. this is to the end.

The Man in the Grey Hat

For most of us, we like the man in the white hat in a fight. We love to see him win the battle over the man in black. But what many of us fail to see is the man in the gray hat. They fail to see him. They fail to see how he is pulling the strings behind the scene. He is the real controller and the referee of the whole fight. He holds the real power and he is the one calling all the important shots. He stands between us all, he instigates the fight and becomes the hero to all when he separates us and calls for peace.

The vast majority of people live in a reserve pool. They are the uncommitted souls in the world. They are led around by those who influence them. They are caught up by the show on stage. They believe that it matters.

The cares of this world have them tied down and enslaved. They are the most uninformed and the most ill informed. They are like the waves of the sea. They are pushed here and there by their emotions. The controllers give their options to them; they have no choice but to believe in them. If they stop believing in them, and question the voice of the controllers, where would they seek their instructions? They have no faith in God. They have left Him and He has left them.

A Sea of People

The puppet masters know that they need the mob for muscle, and from the ranks of the mob come their own enforcers, no one knows the mob better then their own.

They have used and will continue to use the mob day by day.

They are, for the most part, uncommitted souls. But when pushed or stirred up, they are like the sea, they roar and the power of the mob can crush the enemies of the state. That is the source of so much power to the controllers, and they use it well.

Most in the mob are fence sitters. The problem is that they are unaware that the fence is metal, and that we are in an electrical storm. And in this last age, they are in the worst place they can be.

They need to make the right choice or soon, a choice will be made for them. They will either get off the fence themselves or die trying in the coming Tribulation.

Billions will die in the soon coming Apocalypse. They are human cannon fodder and the world elite knew it from the beginning. But they, the mob, feel that they are loved and cared for by their leaders and so they do not know that they are being bought and sold.

The blame for this can be spread around. The information they are given is false from both sides at times. Some are misled, and therefore mislead others. Others are completely deceived and therefore are deceiving others. Still others know what they are dispensing is a lie, and still, they fill the airwaves with it.

The masses flow like a river around the manmade bends in the river of life. They are pushed this way and then that way. They are controlled. They wash themselves in stories of aliens, but turn down the only extraterrestrial knowledge that was ever given to man, the Holy Bible. For what, for fables and fairy tales? But this is meant to be. For few are Called and even fewer are Chosen.

Those on each side of the battle feel their cause is right and their reasons are just. They feel they should and will win in the end. Even the Christian Church is caught up in this world of Politics. Not seeing that the church came in as a Martyr and will go out as a Martyr.

Like Zealots of old, the Old Testament, they have chosen the wrong path, they do not know what spirit they have. They plan to fight to the death. And death they will have.

Liars on both sides

The leaders and speakers of many Patriot and Conspiracy groups have their own agenda, both personal and public. They have their own lusts and needs, their own lust for power and position.

This drives many of them. This is normal and must be remembered in the back of our minds. They have needs like all men and these needs and lusts, they will fulfill. Even if it takes weaving a tale or two, they will do it. Some have imaginations that are overly active, influenced by spirits as well as competition.

They set up camps and fortify themselves against one another, some for petty reasons. They become enemies against one another, more so than against the real foe. They fight small battles while losing the big war. But such is life.

The Coming Social Order

The International movement toward a Global or World State is forever changing the face of America and the World. We are headed for a Global Village. The Globalization movements, one day, will elimate all Nation-States. How will they do this?

By interlocking all the diverse nation-states with international agreements, treaties, laws and debts. The US is the world's most globalized country to date. We are now so interlocked with China that we cannot break free without suffering much economic and political pain.

America is in debt as is most of the world. America has a $250 Billion trade deficit with. How did this come about? In steps, our creditors gave many to a greedy child, and they know that one day they will demand that our debtor nation change its internal laws or else. Then we will have to answer to our new masters, the International Bankers.

We are in a downwards slide with no hope of returning. That was their goal from the beginning that is still their purpose; they do not want us to go back. Their aim is a global welfare state. They want us so interlocked with other nation-sates, that it will be easier to go forward than to go back, this also will make it much easier to move from economic globalization to political globalization.

Now in Lebanon, we see a call for an International Security Force that will bring in a Global armed security force into the region. This push will continue around the world. Later, a call for a fully manned global armed force, which they have been aiming for all along will be wedded and wielded together for bad or worse.

9

But it first had to start with your money. It is with this economic side that they say that they wish to bring in a higher standard of living for the Third World. Some see this movement as the savoir of the poor countries.

They smile while they ship jobs and money away from the western nations. They are bent on a socialized world, one way or another.

They believe that this economic prosperity will one day bring about a social prosperity to these Third World countries. But what we are also seeing now is an Americanism or westernizing of these countries and cultures.

Not with the good side of America, but with our evil ways, these ways are sweeping the globe. It is not the best of America, but the worst. How is this being done? Through our corporate and popular cultural imperialism!

The increasing interdependence and interaction with other nation-states and Non-Governmental Organizations has us bound. The day will come and it is not that far away, when our newspapers, radio stations and churches will have to seek licenses to operate. We will lose our right to own private property and to place soldiers on our own borders.

The day is coming when Global Courts will rule against us and force us to follow the GATT and NAFTA treaties to our downfall. The day is coming when Congress and our state governments will no longer be able to protect us from all harm, both foreign and domestic. That day is now. And that global authority is growing.

Two

Earth -Their Playground

"In the event that I am reincarnated, I would like to return as a deadly virus, in order to contribute, something to solve overpopulation." Prince Philip, Report by Deutsche Press Agentur (DPA), August 1988

The name of their god varies. Some call her, Gayatri, Tiamat, Kubau; others call her-Dana, Rhea, Cybele, Potnia Theron, Demeter, Artemis, Athena, Magna Mater, Ceres, Gaia, Tellus or Terra. In mythology, she is the mother of the gods.

It is said that she brought forth and gave birth to her equal and one of her many mates-Uranus, the sky god. He too has many names.

Who is she, she is Mother Earth, and this is their playground. To the Overclass and to the Super-Elite, we are their chess pieces, the masses to be used as needed. For some of them, it is time to remove the spoilers of their mother. It is time for us to die. We are but parasites to be removed from Mother.

As the Neo-Pagans make their presence known, we will see an increase in Bel/Baal worship in the world. This belief goes back to the days of the Sumerians, Babylonians, Egyptians, Greeks and Romans. Some openly worship the Gaia, whether they believe she is the Earth or the Goddess of the Earth, they worship her. It is not surprising to me to learn that one of her sacred animals is the serpent and the narcotic poppy is seen in her hand.

Gaia took a husband by the name of Uranus, who was also her son. This is the same template as in the story of Semiramis and Nimrod. And as with Uranus, Nimrod was cut into pieces and spread out over the earth.

As with the gods of old, this new pagan religion looks for a Golden Age, yet come. They believe they will have their Utopia, their Paradise here on earth.

But unlike the true Christian, they believe that they must fight for this Utopia, and that they must remove their enemies and the enemies of their mother, from the earth to achieve this.

Some of them also wish to be made immortal, but not all of them. Some of them seek the chthonic power. Therefore, their vows and oaths in the name of Gaia are the most binding of all to them. And they mean to carry out those vows.

They have agenda and their sole purpose for carrying out this religious activity is to create a new world order. Again, this first starts off as an economic global order, which will be a world capitalist-socialist government, and a global Luciferian, Satanist, Wiccan centered religion.

Their goal is to achieve a community of nations, a world government that would make, interpret and enforce the laws of this global government in this new global village.

All nations will be required to surrender their sovereignty. This will add another layer or level of government upon the shoulders of the people of the world.

The elements for this world government are already in place and in play, and their edicts are already being enforced inside the Federal and State governments in the United States of America. This idea is not new. Nimrod founded the first Order out of chaos after the Flood, and God destroyed it.

The Babylonians conquered the known world; the ancient Greeks conquered them and expanded their reach. Then came the Romans and more lands were added, nations and tongue were put under their control. The idea grew with the passage of time.

The idea of a federation of city-states and then nation-states has been with us since before the time of Nimrod. Men have been seeking for the Perpetual Peace in an age of ever-increasing wars; this has brought us to this day and to this time.

This is a time of man seeing himself as a Citizen of the World. In so much that, they are willing to give up their God-given rights of governing themselves and give this right to a nation, or an assembly of nations, to rule over them.

And for this body to elect a man, a superman, that will set order in the world. This shows how man has lost sight of his moral obligation and duty to his God and has placed his nation or his ideas in God's place.

These men think that they can solve their problems and alleviate all their fears by giving this entity, this government, unlimited power, which will in turn give this power over to a mere man and his political and religious office.

He will in turn, punish us when we violate his rules. Their goal, their concepts are: one man, one ruler governing the entire world.

They have begun to regionalize the world, just as the United States of America has regionalized its member states in North America. Just as we grouped together our fifty separate states into a more perfect Union, they too desire the same for the United Nations of the World. As we have done, they desire to do the same to the world.

This truly will help in managing the World Republic. Others call this set up a Global Commonwealth of Nations. This they see as a key to their launching their new religion.

We as a world body have made the steps to meet these requirements. We have a universal system of weights and measurements; we have at this time a common accepted currency for many nations, the U. S. Dollar.

Yes, I believe that there will be a call in the future for a unification of all currency, a global currency. Right now, the American dollar is used the world over. The Euro is coming up strong to one day take its place.

Right now, English is spoken the world over. There will be a call for a global language in the future. You see, things are going to change. How soon? This, I do not know.

Laws and Constitution

"I believe at some future day, the nations of the earth will agree on some sort of congress which will take cognizance of international questions of difficulty and whose decisions will be as binding as the decisions of the Supreme Court are upon us." Ulysses S. Grant

They have been busy bees all over the earth. They will not tire and they will not stop until they have reached their goal. Their planning stages reaches from the International Peace Congresses held in Europe every two years starting in 1843, to the Institute of International Law in 1873, to the Inter-Parliamentary Union in 1886, to the Hague Conferences of 1899 and 1907, to the League of Nations 1919-1938, to the World Constitution and Parliament Association or WCPA in 1958, to the United Nations of today.

The world federalists got a boost in 1992 when they fostered the Maastricht Treaty; this gave then the European Union, or the EU. The EU has expanded to reach 450 million people in 25 member states.

Not to be left behind, the African nations formed the African Union in 2002, and then came the South American Community of Nations in 2004. The Southeast Asian Nations followed this closely.

This shows the rational regional groups. With 191 nations in the UN. They are being subdivided as we speak.

These are examples of incremental establishment of a global federation of Nation-States. This makes the next step that much easier.

The EU has open borders, as does the states within the US. This is also sought in the Americas as we will soon see with the NAFTA agreement between the US, Canada and Mexico.

In 1998, they again leaped forward with the Rome Statute; this led to the establishment of the International Criminal Court in 2002.

Your Pocket

For control of the world, you must have control of the money. They have us there too. You see, they worked that out in the Bretton Woods meeting in New Hampshire, in 1944.

From this meeting came the World Bank and the International Monetary Fund. Now we have the World Trade Organization along with the Organization for Economic Co-operation and Development or OECD. Please do not doubt them, for their plans and their power, and their control reaches very far and wide, and it is still growing.

Then there is the military might to carry out the punishment of the lawbreakers. For that, you have the UN Peacekeepers or regional affiliates like NATO.

Global Declaration of Interdependent

There is a call for world unity. We are being told that our western ideas hold a hollow promise for the rest of the world. That our ideas of comfort and wealth only provoke the extremists in the world to attack us.

What they fail to see is that the world envies us. The liberal socialists of the world now glorify their sins. They want us to surrender for all the wrong reasons. They want us to give up our freedoms and rights for the wrong cause. The liberal socialists are like the Arabs to the Jews, only our death will do.

There are many in the world that see the only hope for world survival is for the rich nations of the world to somehow turn over our wealth and success to the Third World.

But think about it, what would they gain if we did such a foolhardy thing? Nothing! Could they give us a safer and more productive world, no?

It would not be a safer world nor would they secure peace for us or for the Third World. They cannot achieve this by their plans; this world peace that they seek after will not be reached today or tomorrow by giving away the candy store to the neighborhood kids.

On the one hand, the socialists cry out against globalization because the globalized media can now show the world how we live. Then, on the other hand, we are told that we need a more globalized approach of pluralism to solve the world problems, and that America is too myopic. That we need to understand the world though the eyes of our enemies.

In a way, we are and we do need to see ourselves as the enemies see us. For then only will we know what they are capable of.

Do they really have any answers? Are they so envious of America that they are willing to jeopardize the future, our future, for a new international spirit of pluralism?

In their search for a true global democracy, they will only find a true global tyranny. They enjoyed 9/11 and they will enjoy the next attacks upon us even more.

Now as America pushes off its western style materialist world, and as it promotes consumerism to other nations, they too will soon consume energy at the rate, or at a higher rate than that of the US. We are only pushing the world into an energy war.

Soon, these nations will have a veto over our lives and our way of life. They will seek to fulfill their own needs and settle for a world government that will seemingly provide for them. America and the rest of the world will soon choose this dream of a socialist global nation of world unity over true Republican government. This global nation will be built on our graves.

Jeremiah

Now we come to the warnings of God. They are everywhere. And they are for us all. Truly, we are in the Days of Noah and of the Days of Lot once again, some do not believe in God. They will soon see.

Some believe in Him, but believe that He does not care what we do, and there are still others who believe in God, and they know that He cares about us and what we do, yet refuse to yield to God's power, wisdom and mighty hand in their lives. Let us be not like the fools and hear and do the Will of God through the Word of God. Now let us hear about a man of God sent to the people for a warning.

The Book of Jeremiah covers the time period from 627 B.C. to 586 B.C., it was written around 626 B.C. During this time, Judah and Israel began to drift far from God. During this time also, foreign powers began to take control of their land. Their decline continued until the destruction of Jerusalem.

Jeremiah took a brave stand against his people and his own government. But he never rose up to fight against his people or his government with shield and sword; he fought with them, with words, swollen with the will and power of God.

He was a brave man, but he is known as the Weeping Prophet. It broke his heart to see his once great nation on a decline because of sin and disobedience. No one gave him thanks for him calling sin, sin; in fact, he was thrown in to prison as a traitor for talking defeat in a "Time of War".

His message was not popular, nor will ours be either. He dared to speak out without a Freedom of Speech written in his Constitution, what will you do?

Israel as a whole was God's Old Testament Church, and from that group, God pulled out a Bride for Himself. Even before the destruction of Jerusalem, God had promised them that they would be restored back; this was punishment, when the people repented and began to call on God, and He would once again return them to their land. This is not promised to America.

As Christians, we are called to tell the people of the coming destruction. The people must be warned of the coming disaster, this is God's appointed way, first, He warns us, and then He sends destruction upon the land. We are all called to turn from our sinful ways. We must find Christ for ourselves and then tell others the true and perfect way.

This is not easy. Here we have a nation that has gone astray. We as a nation that has lost its character as a Lamb and has taken on the character of a wild beast, a Dragon.

It is hard for us to preach Repentance to the people, but we must, we must find a way. Jeremiah, like many of us, looked upon our own poor wicked frame and told God what he could not do as in Jeremiah 1:6. But God is able to rise up stone to praise Him; surely, He can use a man with life and breathe already in his body.

We must yield as Jeremiah yielded and follow God and His plan as He has laid it out for our lives. Evil men or their power must not intimidate us   men or the power of man. We must preach Repentance. Whether it is to our King (President), Governor, Senator, priests and preachers in the land. For all have gone astray. They have left the Word of God and taken away or added to it. But like in the walk of Elijah, He has some who has not bowed the knee.

Like Jeremiah in his day, we must in our day, see the Day of Judgment going, and go forth and warn the people. For America will continue on its path, it will not turn back; therefore, it is headed straight for death and destruction.

America the Virgin, was espoused to God, it too has turned into a harlot among harlots, and her sins will yet increase ever more. She is degrading herself with many nations and is carrying out injustices in many foreign lands.

This is a prideful and foolish nation, we say that God is on our side, but we truly are not by His side. For we have long ago walked away from God. We have walked away from His Bible and wrote our own; we removed prayer out of our schools and replaced it with condoms.

In the end, we may be the only ones preaching Repentance, in the end, we may have the government and the people against us, but we truly will be standing for and with God and His Word. We must stand, my friends, even if we must stand alone.

What drives them?

The three major things that drive them are what have always driven man, Lust, envy, and self-interest. Three things that they focus on are World population, the Environment, and Energy resources, to name a few. I will focus first on the energy resource, due to the world at war right now in the Middle East. Let us take a look at Hubbert peak oil theory.

Peak Oil

I want this book to be a look into the mirror for us all. I want, I desire, this book to be a way for America to look upon itself and to see the evil that it has done and will do in the spirit of self-interest, lust and envy. What are our real goals, what are our real motives and driving forces behind our actions? I doubt if the American people really knows or cares.

I believe that our leadership will never say what our true goals were for 100 years, or until we have a full Dictatorship in America, and he or she feels free from the shackles of accountability. Then they will let the world in on the quiet little secret. But for now, let us look at the oil crisis.

Let us start with the Hubbert peak oil theory. This refers to a singular event in history where we will one day reach the peak of the whole world's oil production. Then it will be in a decline and run itself out.

This theory comes from an American geophysicist by the name of Marion King Hubbert. He created a model of the known oil reserves in the world and wrote a paper to the America Petroleum Institute in 1956.

This paper covered the continental oil peak and then the global oil peak. In his paper, he stated that the American oil would peak in between 1965 and 1970, it peaked in 1971. Now the global peak may have come and gone as some have stated, for some believed that it peaked in 2005, others have stated that this will occur in 2025. Natural gas is expected to peak by some around 2010 to 2020.

Whether there is a true peak or not, we can truly see the human response to the problem. Control the resources by any means necessary. The Elite in the global market has noted this decline. They know the seriousness of the social and economic factors in the world order. They know that they must remain in control of the last major oil fields. That they must continue the global economic growth, and that they will need cheap energy for this. They know a decline in the oil production will slow or reverse that growth.

One sign of a peak in oil production will be rapidly increasing oil prices, are we seeing this now? Then a worldwide oil shortage would follow. This scenario is not unlike what we are seeing today in the world oil markets. Therefore, demand must be reduced to meet the declining oil supplies.

The world could be seeing less and less produce made from oil. Therefore, in the future, we must find an alternative. Do they, the Elite have one; are they waiting for the right moment to show their hand?

If something does not happen within the next ten or twenty years, we could see a lowering of the living standard worldwide. Look for increases in foodstock and transportation. Watch for the global fight over these very scarce remaining oil supplies. There could be a gradual or an abrupt end to the peak oil supplies worldwide. There could be more wars to be fought. This could lead Russia to make her move against Israel as is foretold in the Bible. This all could end in a Petrocollapse.

The Elite of America saw the problem and they devised an American solution to the problem, and it was the establishment of an American Global Empire.

The Project for the New America Century

"As the 20th century draws to a close, the United States stands as the world's preeminent power. Having led the West to victory in the Cold War, America faces an opportunity and a challenge: Does the United States have the vision to build upon the achievements of past decades? Does the United States have the resolve to shape a new century favorable to American principles and interest?" PNAC

This is an American political think tank based in Washington, DC. It was established in 1997, its goal was to promote American global leadership. The group was a spin-off of the New Citizenship Project, which was funded by the Sarah Scaife Foundation, the John M. Olin Foundation and the Bradley Foundation.

This organization preached American domination in global affairs or Pax Americana, through military, economic, space, and cyberspace power and technology. They believe that it was more than necessary to preserve and extend an international order that is friendly towards the US.

It faces up to the "constabulary" role the US plays in the current world order, however, this role would be used to better shape the security or order in critical regions. Regions that is hostile to American presence and influence in the world. In essence, it wishes to promote America as the answer to the whole world order problem, it would place America in a place to subjugate the world and impose upon the world, an America

Imperial and Globalist agenda. America would continue to expand and dominate the world order for selfish reasons.

They hold a narrow view of the world order problem, they do not see that the more we spend of America's wealth, the more it will erode our economic and financial base; they are willing to do this, just for the chance to expand an imperialistic America agenda throughout the world. In carrying out their plans in the Bush II administration, they have lost a great deal of domestic and international support that is so badly needed in this type of expedition.

They seem to be visionaries in one sense, they were able to see into the future and predict that a "catastrophic and catalyzing event"-like a new Pearl Harbor" would take place and be needed to push forward their ideas and positions. This was from their Rebuilding America's Defenses on page 51. This event came in 9/11 and justified the war in Afghanistan and Iraq. They will reshape the world into the image that they desire, no matter what.

Three

Organized Chaos

"It was not my intention to doubt that the doctrine of the Illuminati and the principles of Jacobinism had not spread to the United States. On the contrary, no one is more satisfied of this fact than I am." George Washington, from a letter in 1790

On September 11th, 2001, the world changed for a lot of us. Like the Kennedy murder, we may never know what truly happened. But we do know that America changed from a Lamb into a Dragon. Now, America stomps its way across the globe.

We are seeing the word of God fulfilled in our eyes. We are seeing the fulfillment of Revelation Chapter 13, for we can clearly see this Beast, America, is leading and subduing the whole world for the first beast in Rome.

The world must have order, for it is truly chaotic right now. Part of the problem is the involvement of the Rich nations into the poorer nations, and they are there for all the wrong reasons.

It is also chaotic, because the poorer nations have not gotten their own house in order. It will not take becoming rich to do so. They are poorer because of past and present racism, nationalism, communism, humanism, socialism, and atheism; etc, etc. Sure, there is more than enough blame to go around. But that will not solve the problems that they have today.

So the world needs a global cop. In walks America. For we love order, and we love law enforcement. And the world needs to know that we will stick our noses and our necks into fights that do not belong to us, just to show how loving and caring we are.

But how did we get here? And what has transformed us from the gentile Lamb Beast into the dreadful Dragon. We are now feared and hated the world over.

We have arrived here on a pack of lies, misfortunes, betrayals, deceptions and arrogance. For years, America's current brand of leadership has planned for this move in Eurasia. So this is no surprise to them.

This is the American century, we have been told. They have planned and plotted and now they are in full operational mode as they implement their plans for a world government with an American style. They think they have succeeded, but God is not mocked. The evil we do, we will answer for.

But you say we need order, peace and protection for ourselves, for the weaker people in the world and for the weaker nations. Someone has to do it. True.

But in a free and open society, what you have to do is allow the people to vote on it, you have to preach it until they support it. What you do not do is plant the lies and carries out the plans that kill innocent people.

You do not betray your once sacred principles. You do not carry out a war overseas and a police action at home that places the government against its own people. But we have.

We were lied to about the 9/11 plotters and operators. And we are being lied to about the war on terror. Why was this done, for the purpose of putting a boot on the necks of the unconverted and the uninitiated!

This has allowed our government to carry out operations against Americas that George Orwell wrote about in 1984. And because of our fear, we were glad. And some still are.

We must lose to win

For many people, especially strong-willed Americans, the very thought of losing or surrendering to an enemy is much too great a sacrifice to make. But that seems to be precisely what

God is leading us to. We have behaved liked biblical Israel and refused to serve God, so God will have us put under bondage of man.

As with Israel and Babylon, our days are numbered. The Fifth Colum is within our fortress. Their goals are not our goals; their purposes are not our purposes. We are being eroded from within. Sin is a cancer and so is treason.

Many Christian are looking for the coming Rapture as an escape. Books and movies make millions by telling the story of the coming troubles. But still few know the life that needs to be lived to go into the Rapture.

The unwelcome and unspeakable truth is that billions will die, and that millions of Americans will be enslaved. Why? Because like Eve, they have believed the Lie. These Christian are like Noah they will go through the Tribulation, they will not be going into the Rapture and the truth is; they know it. They know how they are living. You know yourself; you, unlike most, know that you are not living the life, but a lie.

Then there are the groups that do not even believe in the rapture. They believe that everyone must go through the Tribulation. Still others believe it is our duty to hand over the world and its governments to Christ when He returns. They are wrong.

There is a Rapture going on now and there will be a Rapture take place before the Great Tribulation. There is a Rapture taking place right now. There is always a preparation stage in life.

The Bride of Christ will not have to go through this Judgment, for she has already been judged. But the Church Nominal will.

They seek to place a Christian in every stage of government. From the White House to the United Nations. They leave nothing for chance, or Christ. When He returns, what will He have to conquer? They believe that they must do it themselves.

It must be so. They are to play a role in this New World Order. They must work to form this new government, this global hierarchy, for it will be used to fulfill its proposals and duty in the tribulation of the world.

The world is deceived in believing there is peace without Christ; they will only find a short peace without Him, but much tribulation. The world is busy paving the road to its own destruction.

The World is a Stage

So where do we fit in? Where is our place on this stage? What is our part in this play? Why is America building up a system that will one day destroy it? Could someone please tell me why America is building this Global State?

It has so much more to lose, why is America rushing into this Brave New World Order when everyone that can see seems to think that we are at the Beginning of the End, as a nation and as a world order?

Why are we are now rushing headlong into our Brave New Social Order? You say, I do not see that, but are you really looking, or are you just waiting for the Media to tell you when there is a crisis in your life and that you need to act upon it and act now?

Are you feeding off of the controlled crises that arise and engulf the lives of so many? For most of the world, the answer is, yes.

It seems to me that the Persian Gulf Wars were the final beginning of the New World Order. It foreshadowed the appearing of the system of the Antichrist. He is preparing to take center stage and be the center of the world and of your life. Why? Because that is what you, want.

Within it, we see the shape of things to come as many groups and people prepare for their coming Savior, some call him: The Coming One, the Lord Maitreya, the Dark Lord, the Sun God, the Fifth Buddha, the Lord Krishna, and still others look for the great Imam Mahdi. This was brought out so well in Mr. Ralph Epperson's' book, The New World Order.

The road is paved for the world to fall in step with the anti-Christ. They have rejected the true Messiah, the true and Living God; they will now fall for the false Christ, which will be indwelled by Satan.

The world is searching for peace and praying for a great peacemaker. Everyone is calling for a great world leader to rise up and be the hero. Many have foretold of his coming. The New-Agers put a Social twist to it and proclaimed that his coming would bring peace to the world.

That matches the views of the Communist, Socialist and Humanist in some ways, for they proclaimed the New Man, and spoke of how he would put an end to the suffering of the poor and needy of this World.

They have made the plans; the organizations are put in place for him. The order and systems are organized to take away the wealth from the rich nations and give it to the poor nations. And now in America we can see this in so many different forms.

In Europe, socialism is ten fold in presence and power. The systems are there and they are growing. Things are being primed for the master's hands, the Anti-Christ.

They continue to tell us that we need this new law or that new law. When will the people cry out against these new powers that the State has taken upon itself? We are told that if you do no wrong, you have nothing to worry about. That is not how a free people manage their government.

What many people fail to see is that in the near future, that same law that was used to shut down their enemies will make speaking out against a corrupt government unlawful and illegal, and that it was their own lust for control and power over others that brought down doom upon them.

False Uniting

"God's plan is dedicated to the unification of all races, religions, and creeds. This plan, dedicated to the new order of things, is to make all things new — a new nation, a new race, a new civilization, and a new religion, a nonsectarian religion that has already been recognized and called the religion of "The Great Light." C. William Smith-God's Plan in America

They want to quiet the voice of those that speak out against their ways and their plans. They call these the voices of intolerance and oppression.

They feel that once they have silenced us, that they will be able to unite the diverse cultures, ethnic groups, nations, tongues and peoples of this World, into a loving and caring Global family. Through this, they feel, that they will bring forth a New Age of Peace, an Aquarian Age, an a Age of Enlightenment for all inhabitants of the world.

Then there will come a peace that will embrace all faiths, all races and all colors. Gone would be the days of the racist imperialist Christians nation-states.

For the Christians, these would be the End of Days. From them will arise a new man, he will put an End to Time, as we know it. He will establish his-New Order.

This New World Order, which has been shaped by a Luciferian Conspiracy and manifested by human betrayal and deception, is promised by God to be here.

Most of us have the question in our minds of how soon. But Christ has said that we are to live our lives as if He, Jesus Christ, was coming today. So it does not matter when the Anti-Christ is coming, we need to be awake to hear from Christ every day.

Ecumenism

This movement is playing a key role in setting up the global religion. This will be an occult, satanic, mystic, paganized

Christianity. This movement is bringing the harlot daughters back to the Mother harlot Church. This is bringing in all forms of religions the world over.

This is a uniting of Satan's Bride under the cover of Rome. This is Revelation Chapter 17 being fulfilled. By using the call for social justice, the environment, and global peace, Rome has linked modern man together at the End Time.

This further ensures these pagan believers that their prayers are just as effective with God as any Roman and he is right, for God does not hear them either.

But because of the Roman's liberal religious stand and that of the late John Paul II. The Pope of Rome has become the acknowledged spiritual leader of the world. No matter if the worshipper worships in voodoo, witchcraft or prays to ancestors, they will find a home in Romanism.

This has been the way since Constantine, for the time of his genius plan of uniting the empire under his false religion and politician party; the marrying of paganism with Christianity has produced Romanism. The State and Religion was married once again under his Plan. One of the pioneered groups of this blending of faith has been the Jesuits. We will speak more about them later.

But under the Roman's Ecumenical banner, we will find the brotherhood of man and the Fatherhood of God, which they feel embraces all mankind, rather in their temples, churches or synagogues.

They have stepped into the Charismatic Movement with its Signs and Wonders following, and have deceived the sign seeking Protestant Charismatic church with their false anointing.

The Players

We will be looking at the players on and behind the stage. Who are they? Can we identify them? We will speak about the known persons, who are the announcers for the coming New Country. We will go over what we know about them now, and see if we truly know the truth about these organizations.

Then, we will discuss the various groups and how some of them are seen working together and how some of them are suspected of working together. How do they fit in? How do they work together? What are their goals and missions?

Tyrants

What drove these men and women throughout the ages? A vision, they have an idea of how the world really needs to be run and they want everyone to know that they can and will do it better. They wish to lead us and they will do whatever it takes to win.

They wish to have total control over others. This is the only way they know it will work. Now if we look back into the past, we can see Lucifer trying to remove God from His throne. Lucifer made the challenge. There was a war in heaven and then Lucifer was evicted. He has moved on down through the ages, inspiring man to carry out his plans. So it is today. Let us look to the past, to see the future.

Nimrod

Nimrod was a major player in the world order game. He was a son of Cush, who was a son of Ham, who was a son of Noah. Nimrod became the first notable King, Ruler or Emperor in Mesopotamia after the flood.

In the Bible he is called, "a mighty hunter before the Lord." And "a mighty one on the earth." Now as time passed, the story of the flood was passed down from age to age.

Man supplemented legends and traditions into many of the stories. So it is with the true religion that God has given us.

Man inspired by Satan has polluted the Gospels of God. This we can see in the creation of the Babylonian Mystery Religion in the time of Nimrod. This is the mother of all false religions and Mythologies that would come after.

Here in these beliefs, we see the first Queen of Heaven-Semiramis or Astarte and her son Nimrod or Marduk. The name Marduk was a secret and sacred name.

Here again, we can see Satan corrupting a true mystery of God to confuse mankind. With Nimrod's religion, you had to join his fellowship to learn these mysteries.

The mother and child would later take center stage after Nimrod is killed and reborn as Tammuz. The story is not unlike the worship that is propagated by the Vatican throughout the world.

The names changed as the religion moved from country to country and language to language. So the world is filled with mother and child stories as in Isis and Osiris, Venus and Adonis and now Madonna and child. But to have the false, there had to be a true.

Nimrod seems to be the first leader and Master Builder to pull together a mighty army and secure for him self, an empire. This empire spread from Babylon/Babel, Uruk, Akkad, and Calneh in Sumeria, to Nineveh, Resen, and Rehoboth-Ir, all the way to Calah in Assyria.

From history and the Bible, we get a picture of a man who was religious, powerful and charismatic. His power was renowned.

From his actions, we see the seeds of tyranny planted upon the earth and how tyrants in the future world carry out their plans to enslave the world. First, they need fear, the flood had happened and the story of it was told to each succeeding generation.

So he kept the people fighting past demons. This shows us the lack of man's insight. By building a tower, he was preparing a defense for another flood. He was locking the gate after the sheep had escaped.

It would not protect them from what God had planned for them next. It is the same today, as we fight this so-called war of terror. We are looking in the wrong direction for the enemy.

God always has a champion on stage to provide for his people. That champion was Enoch. Enoch was a master builder also. But his work was for God.

Enoch built the first pyramids, which was a true testament to the true and living god. It was a symbol of the bible upon the earth.

So one built to deceive and the other to reveal. Nimrod built his tower to worship his false gods and Enoch built his pyramid to worship his true God. A struggle of wills ensued, but Nimrod's actions displeased God. He made the people dependent on him. He ruled with a heavy hand.

He gave the people a false purpose and a false hope. All in the name to keep them together. Socialists in our day have done the same.

FDR and Hitler created great works for the people, yet took away many of their rights. They also understand that the people must be entertained. Unity comes with a cost.

It is said that Shem, a son of Ham, later killed Nimrod for his evil ways.

And his body was shipped around the known world. But before that, Nimrod had married his mother, Semiramis. She was famed for her beauty, voluptuousness and her alluring power. They were later worshipped as mother and child.

Tyrants love wars. The Babylonia god Marduk was associated with the planet Mars, a god of war. With their lust for power, they will seek to conquer more and more lands, all the while showing the people their charming side. Nimrod, as many tyrants do, sought to be worshipped, that was the spirit of the Devil working in him.

They desire to play God in our lives. He became the Vicar of God on the earth, and then a god himself.

In the book of Genesis, we have a book of beginnings. Here we see the seed of the anti-Christ. In the book of Revelation, we have the full-grown man and his spirit guide. Now from this seed we have seen grow a multitude of forests. For the anti-Christ must have his army, as does the devil.

Man was created to fellowship and worship God. Satan knows this; therefore, he has inspired many religions to counterfeit the true fellowship and worship of God. God started his revelations in the heavens. He wrote His first Bible there.

Therefore, Satan has made his first strike there. We went from true and pure Astronomy to Astrology, the false and corrupt view of heaven and earth.

God created the heavenly bodies and its pure knowledge, Satan has come along and perverted it. That has been and will ever be the mode of operation for Satan.

Satan's religions have been a controlling and unifying factor in mankind's history. He has built these religions and placed himself at their center.

We see the rise of Nimrod as a High Priest and Pontiff Maximus to the people. He was their only way to heaven.

By using the fear of the people for another flood, he was able to bring them together as one group with one voice, they were one.

And upon this pyramid or tower, was his great observatory built. God saw their work and He was not pleased, He did not approve. So God struck them with Tongues of Confusion.

And so it is today in many religions. Their unity was broken. Mankind broke up into many tongues, people and nations. Even until this day, there is not one language spoken universally, I would say English comes close.

In the Babylonian religion, we see the rise of the Serpent and the Dragon symbol. Here they are worshipped. The Dragon was Nimrod's personal emblem.

Now many do not believe in the anti-Christ. But we see the first-born man reject and resist the will of God and kill his brother. We can plainly see that this seed is the anti-Christ seed, led by Satan, the anti-Christ spirit. That is how far back this war goes, right back to the beginning. And it will not end until, like Abel, the sons of God are removed from upon the face of the earth. But not all will be removed like Enoch and Elijah. All to show the glory of God.

Now notice, Satan is not the Serpent, but he is the spirit that possesses and inspires the Serpent in the Garden. He is the indwelling spirit that guided the Serpent to tempt Eve. Satan is not the Anti-Christ, but he is the spirit of the Anti-Christ. And in the end, he will come down and fully posses the man. As God filled Christ in His every being after the Water baptism, so will Satan fill the Anti-Christ after a certain time!

Satan as the prince of the power of the air, the god of this age, the lord of the rebellion and the lord of the black void of the north will have complete control of the earth and its entire people. God set all of creation in order; Satan plans to place all in disorder and disarray.

His hour and day is coming, but not yet. God has laid out the struggle from Genesis to Revelation and has written it out in the heavens as a witness to man. Are you reading the real and true signs?

Pythagoras

Pythagoras was born 565 B.C., on the Island of Samos. He was the founder of the mystic, religious and scientific society called Pythagoreans.

This was a secret religious society. Today, Pythagoras is considered a prophet by the Ahlu l-Tawhid or Druze faith, along with Plato.

Pythagoras was said to have been taught by Pherekydes. From this belief system, it is believed to be the origin of the use of the pentagram.

His father was a wealthy merchant. He traveled abroad with his father many times. Pythagoras finally made it to Memphis, Egypt, where it is said that he came up with the idea of forming his own religious rites and beliefs; this later began the Pythagoras cult. There in Egypt, he also learned Mathematics, Philosophy, and Astronomy.

He returned to Samos and founded a school. He named this school the Semi Circle.

He was later thrown into jail for speaking his mind to the king, sometime later he was released, but banished from the Island. He moved to Croton in southern Italy where he founded a society to match his beliefs.

There in this group, all men and women were equal. Of his followers, there consisted two groups, an inner circle and an outer circle. The inner circle was the elite, and lived within the compound; they held no private property and were vegetarians.

They were called "Mathematikoi" (mathematicians). The "Akousmatics" (listeners) were the outer circle. They lived in the general community and were allowed to own personal possessions.

Both groups were bound by a strict pact or code of secrecy regarding all activity within the society. Pythagoras described himself as a semi divine person.

Isaac Long

As time went on, great men with their great minds die, but their beliefs lived on in others. In the correct time and season, along came Isaac Long.

Mr. Long moved to Charleston, South Carolina and helped set up the Ancient and Accepted Scottish Rite. He brought with him a statute of Baphomet. Charleston, being located on the 33rd parallel of latitude, was a perfect spot for him. Baghdad is also on the 33rd parallel.

What he had created was the Mother Supreme Council of all Masonic Lodges of the World. As time went on, he died and Albert Pike succeed him and changed the order to the New and Reformed Palladian Rite or Reformed Palladian.

Albert Pike

On 29 December 1809, Albert Pike was born in Boston. He went to college at Harvard. He later fought in the Civil War and after the war. He was tried and convicted of treason. But was later pardoned by President Andrew Johnson, who was a fellow Freemason. President Johnson, on 20 June 1867, was conferred his fourth (4th) 32 Degree of the Scottish Rite. Reminds me of the pardons of President Clinton.

Mr. Pike later established the framework for setting up the plans for many organizations that would run the New World Order. In his day, he began to engineer and plan for the world order. These plans, I believe, are being followed even today.

Let us look to see what could have got him started on his journey? Mr. Pike said that he had a vision. And this vision allowed him to write a blueprint of the events that have begun to run their course in the 20th and 21st Century. All this gave from a 19th Century man. In these plans, we see wars that are set to hammer and shape the world into the image that they desire!

It has been said that Pike was a genius, and that he could read and write in 16 different languages. Not unlike Pope John Paul II, for he could speak 12 different languages. Pike was a 33rd degree Mason. And a Grand Master of the Luciferian order of the Palladium or Sovereign Council of Wisdom. This group was founded in Paris, in 1737.

Pike became the Grand Commander of the North American Freemasonry from 1859-1891. It is also said of Pike that he was a member of the Knights of the Klu Klux Klan; he was also a Satanist and an occultist.

You can see this in his writing. In 1871, he wrote a Masonic handbook.

Pike also established the Supreme Council in Rome, Italy. Pike later set up 23 subordinate Councils around the world. These branches are reportedly secret headquarters for the Illuminatis. Pike wrote the Morals and Dogma in 1871. Here are some examples of his writings.

"Every Masonic Lodge is a Temple of religion; and its teaching are instructions in religion...Masonry, like all religions, all the mysteries, hermeticism and alchemy, conceals its secret from all except the adepts and sages, or the elect, and uses false explanations and misinterpretations of symbols to mislead...to conceal the truth, which it calls light, from them, and to draw them away from it...the truth must be kept secret, and the masses need a teaching to their imperfect reason...every man's conception of God must be proportioned to his mental cultivation, and intellectual power, and moral excellence, God is, as man conceives Him, the reflected image of man himself."

"The true name of Satan, the Kabalists say, is that of Yahveh reversed; for Satan is not a black god...Lucifer, the Light Bearer! Strange and mysterious name to give to the spirit of darkness! Lucifer, the son of the morning! Is it he who bears the light... doubt it not."

Phileas Walder

Now when Pike began setting up his groups and organizations, he needed help.

That help came from men like Phileas Walder of Switzerland; he became a chief lieutenant of Albert Pike.

His background was varied, for he once was a Lutheran minister, a Masonic leader, occultist, and a spiritualist.

Giuseppe Mazzini

Pike's reach was global. He had help from Mr. Mazzini, who was born in Genoa, Italy in 1830. Mr. Mazzini was a member of the Carbonari, this was a secret association.

And it is said that he was a 33rd degree Mason. It is also said that he later became head of the Illuminati in 1834 and founded the Mafia in 1860.

Pike established the Supreme Council in Rome, Italy; Mazzini led this. But he also set up subdivisions; Lord Henry Palmerston in London, England led one subgroup. And another sub group was in Berlin, which was led by none other than Bismarck.

The Groups

Now as we continue to look at the many different groups that play a part in this global crime order, please remember that some are in it for the money, others are in it for the glory and still others are in it for the ideas and idealisms that their group or party promotes.

But take note; for it seems that those that are involved in these plans are more than willing to do anything to win. And that this attitude is now a part of the American way. We see it in the wars we fight and the way we now treat our prisoners, both foreign and domestic. When you leave God behind, you also leave His morals and His Commandments behind.

Cult of Satan

We have been looking at people; now let us see what is it that makes up these groups? Where do they get their ideas and concepts? Let us look. The Cult of Satan had moved from Egypt to Greece by Pythagoras in the Fifth century.

It is said to have moved from the inner circle of the Masonic Lodges, which were aligned with the Templars. These groups brought the Seat of Satan to the West. They were willing to learn any knowledge. They were willing as was Saul to go to the witch of Endor to hear something from God. This is not unlike our military of today. They have had many programs that searched for answers in the paranormal world.

Here we see what makes up our modern day tower of Babel. Please remember the roots of these groups and organizations. Their focus is in the worship of Satan or Lucifer. And this will be the religion of the future, but it will be hidden, it will be under a different name for the people to rally around.

The Baha'i

"In the destruction of the old world order and in the chaos of these modern times, the work of the new creation is going forward; the task of reconstruction, leading to a complete reorganization of human living..." Alice Bailey, the New International Order

The Baha'i (meaning "glory or splendor") Faith is a religion founded by Bahaullah in the 19th century, in Persia, and it is an International Community that has spawned into a non-governmental organization an NGO, one of its goals is to bring about the global membership of all nations into a global government.

It has offices in Haifa, Paris, Geneva, Addis, Ababa, Bangkok, Nairobi, Rome, Santiago, and Vienna. Its goal is to establish the One Country, a United Federated Global Nation.

Their ideas and activities are high and lofty ones. They sound like ideas that we all should rally for and support that is until you learn their motives behind these activities.

Here are some of their stated goals. They want to foster grass-roots participation in sustainable development initiatives to advance the status of women, to educate children, to prevent drug abuse, to eliminate racism, and to promote human rights education. In other words, they seek to create a utopian world. They seek everlasting peace on earth.

They want Oneness of humanity, order in the world, and an organic change of the structure of our modern society. They want to galvanize the collective will of the world population to overcome barriers to peace.

What all this means is that they want to remove the so-called unwarranted disparity between the rich and the poor. To accomplish this, they say that the rich nations must give away their wealth to the poor nations. This sounds reasonable.

They say that it is time for the rich western nations, the middle class really; for it would be the middle class that would be called upon to foot the bill. The middle class would have to pass on their wealth to nations that are ill prepared to receive these funds.

Then they want a universal, controlled education system, this educational system will promote the essential unity of science and religion. My question is whose religion and whose science. This will be a UN directed education.

They call for an International auxiliary language and script to be adopted and taught in all schools, this program is worldwide, and this, they say, will foster the unity of all mankind.

If you look at this group closely, you will see that it has a lot of power for its small membership, it only has five million people, but they have a very long reach.

It is an NGO at the United Nations; it is also a member of an association, which democratically elects a national governing body, this body is known as the national Spiritual Assemblies.

The Baha'i history shows its involvement with international organizations as far back as the League of Nations in 1926. In 1945, it was there for the UN Charter signing in San Francisco. In 1948, it registered with the UN as an International non-governmental organization (NGO).

In 1970, it was granted consultative status at the UN. Now this status has been deemed special consultative status with the UN's Economic and Social Council (ECOSOC).

This status has further moved into the United Nation Children's Fund (UNICEF) in 1976, then in 1989, this status went to the United Nation Development Fund for Women (UNIFEM), and it has established a working relationship with the World Health Organization (WHO).

The list goes on. So does their sway into your life. But you say, 'What does that matter, why should I care?'

Why, because they view the head of the Vatican as our only hope for making a lasting peace. And they view him as a Global spiritual leader.

The Vatican has that same view and desires to be the spiritual leader of the world. And one day it will be, where will you end up, will you be in the inner circle, the outer circle or cast out?

Their First Step is always to create and then Control the Supermarket!

"A supranational authority to regulate world commerce and industry; an international organization that would control the production and consumption of oil; an international currency that would replace the dollar; a world development fund that would make funds available to free and Communist nations alike; an international police force to enforce the edicts of the New World Order." Brandt Commission-Fifth Socialist International, 1991.

Four

The Elite

Elitism with its attitudes and beliefs is cemented into our culture. Neither this idea nor its ideals are new to us. We call someone with a specialized training or education in his/her field an expert. We vote for the most educated, and for the offspring of the best families.

The elites are presented to us and are chosen by us, as the best able to govern our nation. The elite status is an entitlement to better treatment and a better way of life, the rich and the famous do not have to live up to the same standards as we are held to.

The Oligarchies that rule America pull their leaders from the American Aristocracy. These small but dominant groups run America; they are the seed of the European's elites for the most part. They enjoy a status of power and wealth we will never see. They are the privileged few.

As Christians, we are to be humble, neither their wealth nor their position should be envied by us, for that is a sin that we need not add to our growing pile.

We just need to know, and to watch, as well as pray as we observe the role that they have to play in this game. For many of them, this will be their greatest hour, what awaits them in the afterlife is only torment, in a pitiless and bottomless hell. In that hell, they will find the rich and the famous alongside the penniless and poor man.

Once the blue blood elites arrives at the top, it does not stop there. He wants to be elite among elites. Now some blue blood may fall on hard times. But even if they end up penniless, their blue blood status would speak for them to the lower classes, and when the time came, someone with new money on their way up would intermarry into the old money, as some of the English blue bloods do, for they still marry for titles. They rule from generation to generation.

The elite in our society come from many different categories; there are the religious elites, the class elites, the financial elites, the academic elites, the entertaining elites, and the military elites. Now, one born in the upper crust of the society can be in several categories at the same time.

One son of an elite clan can join the military and rise in rank, taking on power that is more direct for himself and his family name. While another son of the same elite family clan could join the priesthood and rise in rank also, both would be holding class and positional elite status. As it was done in biblical times, so is it done today!

What have they gained for it? As the dominant classes in America, they have easier access to more money and political power. While we are being indoctrinated in our public schools, they are receiving an education that will be placing them in positions to direct, rather than follow the norms. The elites are trained and educated to govern the indoctrinated skilled masses, the mob.

Some would say that we have always been a society based on genetic and racial status, rather than a county that promotes based on merits. It is the high born club and group members that will get into the inner circles, all else will remain on the sidelines, until needed, or to fill a token role.

With the advent of racial pseudoscientific research, the elite of today feel justified in their right to power and money, they feel that they are the blue bloods and they are superior in every way that matters.

The Globalist

Their Plan is to control the whole world with a global government. There is to be a United Federation of Nations, in this world governing body, they would rule through three established supranational institutions. They will have an Executive, Legislative and Judicial branch. No one would be accepted from membership in this Federation, membership will be mandatory and universal. I can see the American Civil War as an example of physical force that would be employed to maintain cohesion and order.

Once established, the control of the global society would then fall into the hands of a very select few in this supranational organization. Unlike America, I see a system that elects it supreme leader from its members. I do not foresee any direct elections by the people. In the near future, the United Nations Charter will be revised and codified for the rearrangement of power in the world.

If you watch the news, you can see America as the bully pushing other nations around because of its size. When will the world tire of us and call for a more multilateral approach for world problems? Could this be the reason for our behavior? Those that desire the global agenda, could they be applying a reverse course to get to where they wanted to be in the first place?

Now this global government would have complete access to all governing states. It would monitor and enforce disarmament of all nation-states. There will be no greater military power than this Global Government. This will be a global force. It will have sea, air, and land and space forces. These forces will have a normal operational level of 500,000 troops; the members of this army will be drawn from many nations.

They will be wearing the United Nations uniform. It will have the only allowed nuclear armed forces. It will settle all disputes among the lesser powers, and keep the peace among the nations. For them to have the manpower to do this, the UN will have global taxing authority.

As in the United States, all other powers would be reserved to the lesser nation-states. And as it is here, the Federal Government would soon take even that away.

This global system will be an all reaching and all-powerful entity, there will be no exceptions. It will have a monopoly of power. The 'United Nations' as we now know it will soon change into what they have always wanted it to be. The Final Authority.

Many have spoken of this. One such voice was Lincoln P. Bloomfield, a CFR member. He wrote a study called: "A World Effectively Controlled by the United Nations." This study was commissioned by the State Department in 1962, the contract number was scc2870. You can find this quoted in Global Tyranny-Step by Step, by William Jasper.

Centralization of Control

We are a nation of debt slaves. But we were warned, we have been told to owe no man anything but love. Instead, we have created holidays of greed; Christmas is nothing more than a day of indulgences. Our money is based on nothing, and daily we create more and by creating more, we further this problem.

No one really saves in America but the rich, if we all did, this nation of greed would collapse. But from its ashes would arise a debt-free people. Do not worry, it will not happen.

They have thought out each move, they have planned this out very well. As in the days of Joseph, they have it well planned; there will come a Financial, Agricultural and a Political collapse in the world. And since we have become an indebted nation, the private now owns us banks and global institution that lends us their money. Therefore, we will fall prey as many other nations have before us.

When we borrow funds like all other nations, the funds will have conditions in which we will agree to. Then from there on, we must continue to meet those conditions if we are to stay free in the future. Who can help us? The politicians are powerless, even if they have a good heart; they do not have the knowledge or the understanding to get us out of these problems.

And now we have enslaved ourselves in the global Economic order. Next, we will be enslaved in the Political order and finally, we will be enslaved in the Religious order.

There is nothing that you can do. Our only hope, the only hope for the world, is in Christ. Our higher institutions of justice have been bored out; they too lack any real power. They are only there to makes us feel that our opinions counts for something.

Therefore, we must still pray for our leaders in this country and now for our global leaders, for they are destined to lead us. And they will need our prayers. For we all know that God is still in control, and He will lead us and guide them. But there is coming a day when they will act against us, still we are Christians. If not, now is the time to be one.

They have sold our country right from under our feet. They can and they have taken land from private citizens of the United States and turned it over to another. All in the name of the state. They have and will restructure our government to give themselves more power and more authority. Soon we will have to ask for permission to write a book, to go to church and to preach the Word of God.

They will allow major corporations to grow even bigger, making huge Trusts in America and the world. America will be owned by outside entities. And they will make it a criminal offense to speak against their illegal, unjust and unethical behavior.

A Global Government is their aim and they will reach it, the question is when and how. By how I mean, will you be left alive or killed off for them to get their universal house in order?

Into a few hands will go much more power. We can see this in the merger madness as it continues to sweep the land. The plan is working well. From telecommunication, to carmakers, to farm and farmland. Things are on the move. We as a people are losing even our public water rights. What more is to come? I guess we will have to wait and see. Now it is time to ask the question, who has done this to us and what is their plan? Can you stand the truth, I do not think so.

The Jesuits

The Jesuits have been a major player on the global stage for a very long time. They have been in the political and religious arena since their creation in 1539. Officially, the group is called the Society of Jesus. They are a community of Fathers, that is, ordained priests and Brothers who are not ordained. There are over 20, 000 Jesuits in the world today.

Their founder was Ignatius of Loyola. He came from a proud Basque noble family. At the siege of Pamplona, he was wounded in battle. During his recovery, it is said that he had a remarkable transformation of his life. He began reading the histories of the saints. When he recovered, he became a pilgrim and traveled as far as the Holy Land.

Later in his spiritual development, he began to use Spiritual Exercise as a guide. Not unlike the Buddhist and Mystics of the East. He later gave his Spiritual Exercises to about seven or ten of his friends.

They founded a new order. This new order would be different from most. For the whole world would be its cloister. The new order spread across the entire world.

Their Vows

Now the Jesuit vow is not unlike the Oath of the Illuminati, Knights of Columbus, Knights of Malta and Rhodes Scholars. In fact, some believe that these vows are based on the Oath of the Jesuits. So I will cover in this section only the Jesuit vow.

Now like the other Catholic Orders, the Jesuits take the traditional vows of religious life; chastity, and poverty. However, the Jesuits also take a fourth vow of obedience to the Pope, for special missions. Some say that there is a secret vow that the Jesuits take also. This will be discussed later.

This Order has a turbulent history, to say the least. It is said to have entangled it self in and encouraged many conflicts. The most famous of these was the Reductions in Latin America.

Hmmm, now we have the Renditions in our day, these operations are run by a Catholic controlled government and secret government agency, which is itself controlled by Catholics.

The Reductions was portrayed in the movie: The Mission. The conflicts grew until its abolition in 1773. It was later re-instituted in 1814. As with President Kennedy and his efforts to abolish the CIA, the Mafia, and the Federal Reserve, Pope Clement XIV took the action to abolish the Jesuits in July 1773; after this action, he soon died.

A Jesuit is trained to be a single cell. He learns to work and live alone. He must show that he has the inner and physical strength. Along with the mobility to service anywhere in the world on a new mission when the call is made. You can receive this same information from the Jesuits on the Netherlands and Flanders Jesuit web site. The opinions are mine.

Elevation of the Neophyte

When a Jesuit that is of a low rank is to be elevated to a higher command, he is brought into the chapel of the Order. There, he will find three others present. The principal or Superior will be standing in front of the altar.

On both sides of the altar, he will find a monk. One of them will be holding a yellow and white banner. These are the papal colors. The other will hold a black banner with a dagger and a red cross above the skull and crossbones. The candidate kneels at a red cross placed on the floor.

At this time, the Superior hands the candidate a black crucifix while at the same time he presents him with a dagger. The candidate grasps the crucifix with his left hand and presses it to his heart. The candidate holds the dagger by the blade with his hand as the point of it is placed against his heart. The Superior holds onto the hilt while addressing the candidate:

The Superior says:

"**My son, heretofore you have been taught to act the dissembler: among Roman Catholics, to be a Roman Catholic, and to be a spy even among your own brethren; to believe no man, to trust no man.**

Among the Reformers, to be a reformer; among the Huguenot, to be a Huguenot, among the Calvinist, to be a Calvinist; among the Protestants, generally to be a Protestant, an obtaining their confidence, to seek even to preach from their pulpits, and to denounce with all the vehemence in your nature our Holy Religion and the Pope; and even to descend so low as to be a Jew among Jews, that you might be enabled to gather together all information for the benefit of your Order as a faithful soldier of the Pope."

"You have been taught to insidiously plant the seeds of jealousy and hatred between communities, provinces, states that were at peace, and incite them to deeds of blood, involving them in war with ach other, and to create revolutions and civil wars in countries that were independent and prosperous, cultivating the arts and sciences and enjoying the blessings of peace. To take sides with the combatants and to act secretly with your brother Jesuit, who might be engaged on the other side, but openly opposed, to that with which you might be connected, only that the Church might be the gainer in the end, in the conditions fixed in the treaties for peace and that the end justifies the means."

"You have been taught your duty as a spy, to gather all statistics, facts and information in youth power from every

source; to ingratiate yourself into the confidence of the family circle of Protestants and heretics of every class and character, as well as the of the merchant, the banker, the lawyer, among the schools and universities, in parliaments and legislatures, and judiciaries and councils of state, and to be all things to all men, for the Pope's sake, whose servants we are unto death."

"You have received all your instructions heretofore as a novice, a neophyte, and have served as a co-adjurer, confessor and priest, but you have not yet been invested with all that is necessary to command in the Army of Loyola in the service of the Pope. You must serve the proper time as the instrument and executioner as directed by your superiors; for none can command here who has not consecrated his labors with the blood of the heretic; for "without the shedding of blood no man can be saved." Therefore, to fit yourself for your work and make your own salvation sure, you will, in addition to your former oath of obedience to your order and allegiance to the Pope, repeat after me:"

The oath appears in the book-The Suppressed Truth about the Assassination of Abraham Lincoln, by Burke McCarty, pages 14-16. You can find this information at the Bible Believers web site on the Jesuits. As the ceremony continues, the candidate is then asked several questions.

Question: Who commands you?
Answer: The Successor of St. Ignatius Loyola, the founder of the Society of Jesus or the Soldiers of Jesus Christ.
Question: Who received you?
Answer: A venerable man in white hair.
Question: How?
Answer: With a naked dagger, I kneeling upon the cross beneath the banner of the Pope and of our sacred order.
Questions: Did you take an oath?
Answer: I did, to destroy heretics and their governments and rulers, and to spare neither age, sex nor condition.

> To be as a corpse without any opinion or will of my own, but to implicitly obey my Superiors in all things without hesitation of murmuring.

Question: Will you do that?
Answer: I will
Question: How do you travel?
Answer: In the bark of Peter the fisherman.
Question: Whither do you travel?
Answer: To the four quarters of the globe.
Question: For what purpose?
Answer: To obey the orders of my general and Superiors and to execute the will of the Pope and faithfully fulfill the conditions of my oaths.

Superior says: "Go ye, then, into all the world and take possession of all lands in the name of the pope. He, who will not accept him as the Vicar of Jesus and his Vice-regent on earth, let him be accursed and exterminated."

Now to me, this is somewhat similar to the questions and answers in the Book 1984. The source for this quote is the Bible Believers and other web sites. The opinions again are mine.

Five

Scene One, Act I
The Warning

Brother William Marrion Branham, a man sent from the presence of God, saw a vision in 1933. From this vision, he predicted that a major event would take place by 1977.

This would even be a dark and dismal day for America. Here is what I have learned and what took place in the world around that time.

The Men

In July of 1977, the New Agers were proclaiming that their Lord Maitreya had descended from his ancient retreat in the Himalaya Mountains and had moved into the Asian community in East London, England. They were now trying to call forth their false Christ.

Jimmy Carter was now President of the United States. He was a member of the newly founded Trilateral Commission and a student of his National Security Advisor Zbigniew Brzezinski a co-founder with David Rockefeller of TC.

The Script

On 30 January 1976, Senators and House members were signing The Declaration of Interdependence. The cast in the play was moving along as written. The American super elite were doing away with the nation-state and creating a global one. A Federation of nations was being instituted for the world.

The Seat of Power

The Bible says, "...In the mouth of two or three witnesses shall every word be established." II Corinthians 13:1. For the most part, they have bore witness of themselves; we just have to connect the dots. Please note that I do not pretend to portray this book as having all the answers. What I have presented here is Prophecies and facts. You must draw your own conclusion. However, in life I have found so many people that are not willing even to look.

That the Illuminati's agenda comes from the Vatican is an easy connection for me. But for too many, the fear of looking into the eye of the dragon is too much. They fear that they will see their own reflection.

But what you will find by looking into the pit of its eyes is the Red Demon. Many will still not look. Therefore, they cannot be made aware of the falling hammer to come. The proof is there, but none dare look.

The word Illuminati is the plural of the Latin word, Illuminatus, which means, "One who is Illuminated." For our purpose let us say, that it means a person who has received the full extent or a special knowledge and one who has taken part in a special initiation.

I say that in America today, the Illuminati and their subgroups, Masons, Skull & Bones, and Opus Dei control the Federal government.

They have seized power though the CFR and Trilateral Commission. The Vatican then controls the Illuminatis, which is full of wicked and evil men. Virgin America has been made desolate. She is in bed with all the kings of the world and they are in the hands of the Vatican.

They have and are using the United Nations to destroy the sovereignty of the United States and to enslave the American people. They have been able to conceal this because of their control of all mass media; it is a control that covers television, radio, the press and Hollywood.

And they have infiltrated all opposition forces, and have either destroyed them or defaced them from the inside and from without. They use people; they use our prejudices towards one another to divide us.

They use our hatred for one another. For some hate the Jew, some hate the whites, and still others hate the blacks. They keep us at each other's throats and that is not hard to do.

They have turned each group against the other, making it impossible for them to unite against the real foe. For the most part, this is not hard.

Our fallen human nature is easily used by the devil to do the work. It is their fight against the Bible that has stood out and still does. They are the enemy of the Word of God.

Their Plan is of their father the Devil. It is a plan to be in complete control and to have complete power. Their Plan is to control the U.N. and to have the U.N. control the world. World government is their goal and their only answer. They have the plan and will establish and maintain the supranational institutions with a mandatory and universal membership.

They will employ physical force to get compliance. This will place the complete control of the many in the hands of a few.

The power structures are now being rearranged; the U.N. Charters is being reinforced. The US and Russia are disarming per the treaties set up after World War II. The U.N. will be given, if it does not have already, the resources and the power to inspect and disarm all member nations.

It will be given the political statute in the world to carry out its will upon all lesser states. North Korea, Iran, Iraqi and the U.S. are the test bed of this world body.

Fear Controls

There seems to be a continued flow of information to keep the people ready and on edge for an Alien invasion. Day after day, year after year, the people are fed lies and rumors about government alien projects.

Now, the technology is there, but whose techno is it, and where did it come from? It is the technology of Noah's day, not of E.T.'s. As they have seized power through many roads, they have seized the technology.

The secret Shadow Government holds onto power by limiting our knowledge. From pure science to everyday criminal investigations. By the time, they reveal it to us; it is twenty years old and has already been replaced.

All roads lead to Rome, and the only true political power and authority left upon the earth is the in Rome. They have more spies deployed in America and the rest of the world than we could ever hope for. But must people miss this. This is hidden in plain sight.

The people of Rome, I am not speaking of them, they are many and diverse in views and beliefs. But I am talking of that Mother Church. It is at the top of the pyramid that we find the wicked and evil men.

It is not the common and every day Masons or Roman. They are in danger just as much as I am. It is the invisible elite of whom I am speaking and everyone that stands against the Love of God.

Virgin America

America has told the world of its fight in Iraq. We will go as low and as immoral as we can. The terrorists now set our moral and legal standards.

For we will break any law and any moral code to justify our end. America has allowed herself to be tempted in the dirty games of life and it seems so hard to turn back.

America is being raped by her sister nations and by those called on to guard her. We have allowed the Constitution to be torn to pieces for fear of attacks.

Under President Reagan, we returned to the master's bed of Rome. President Lincoln threw out the Pope's ambassador,

President Reagan opened the gates and let the Trojan Horse of Rome back in.

We are slowly giving up our sovereignty as a nation and our freedom as a people. For what? For temporary peace and pleasures. Their actions have been concealed up to now because of their control of the Mass Media.

They have infiltrated all the major Opposition Forces and have either defaced them, defamed them or destroyed them. They have used the government to monitor and harass them; they have used racism and fear to control them.

This is being done while the people and groups lose themselves in infighting and group envy and hatred. We all must take a little of the blame for the overwhelming success of the Order.

Throughout the history of the Vatican, we can see a trail of blood. From Pagan Rome to Papal Rome, Christians have suffered and died. Papal Rome has taken on the tactics of the carnal world and has left the spiritual life to enter the mystic world.

It has stopped at nothing to further its goals, the conquest of the world, and the subjection of every people, nation and tongue under the sun. No one was safe under the Caesars of Rome, and so it was in the days of the Pope and the Holy Roman Empire.

Even to our own modern day, not even a revolutionary pope like Albino Luciani was safe from the back stage handlers. Luciani had gained power in a reshuffle within the Vatican. He was headed in a new and dramatic direction.

Like JFK, Luciani was planning to remove some powerful men from power. A total of six men, all Freemasons, were in his sights for a purge. According to David A. Yallop in his, book In God's Name: An Investigation into the Murder of Pope John Paul I, the pope found over 100 Masons within the Holy City. There they ran an illegal Masonic Lodge, the P2. It included

Priests, Bishops and Cardinals. Luciani wanted it removed; he knew that it was a curse to his Church.

His nemesis was Licio Gelli, referred to by some as the 'Il Burattinaio' the Puppet Master. His puppets were in many places and several nations. He controlled a lot. The purge would hurt him and the power he held over Rome. There was much to fear. On 28 September 1978, a course of action was taken to remove a problem. It worked.

Control by Conflict

It has been said that Racism is a mental Illness. Then the world is ill indeed. Hatred of others because of their race, gender, color, shape, or size is a sin. Some people seem to be born hateful. Others have been taught and trained.

Across the entire world, hatred and mistrust are on an all time high. Satan uses people and groups to further his aim. In the late 20th Century, the only true friend of Israel was nominal Christian America.

But there is both love and hate for Israel in America. The world at large has not stood for the state of Israel in their times of trouble, why? Are they hated for being so strong in a weak region?

Are they hated for standing on their faith while others sold theirs? In the Conspiracy world, we see this ethnic group/race being used as a scapegoat by the bigots and race baiters.

America is playing a role, a necessary role, in keeping Israel as a nation-state. But one day soon, neither America nor Israel will be needed to carry on its role, as the glue that holds the world order in place will be gone.

The world needs something to hate. Hate gives people focus, energy and purpose. The world at large hates and envies America and Israel.

One day, they will have their wish and see the destruction of America and Israel. In the end, God will judge all nations.

It was the Jews that took the blunt of the Jesuits-led army in Germany during World War II. This was pure hatred that brought forth such murderous lust. Yes, the founder of the Illuminati was a Jew, but he was a Romanized Jew. They have used the Jews and the Jewish community the world over as the focus of their hate.

Yes, we see Jews coming into power and money the world over, for they are blessed. In every race, you will and do have evil people. So also with the Jews, the Israelite is no different from any other man, some were evil.

Nevertheless, we can find evil in every race. When you label a race as wicked or evil, you only show how wicked and evil you are. It is not the race, but individuals that commit sins.

Nevertheless, with the Racist mind, the brush is wide and the acts of a few cover the entire race. For those that were in the Conspiracy, they may have been Jewish, but many other ethnic groups were there also.

Their Religion was Roman or even Protestants. Their Masonic Rituals and/or the Atheist beliefs governed their acts. From the Great Whore of Rome I believe comes the influence, they have control of the World Conspiracy.

Not only for the Romanized Jew, but also for all that fall under the sway of the Whore in Rome. They used the Jewish people like they use the rest of us, and then they preach the hate. Instead of hate and envy, I see in the Jewish Community the blessing of God in the natural as well as in the spiritual.

In Science, Finance, Medicine, Military Power and World Government, the Jewish people excel, and they are hated for it. But in each race, we have the used and the users. We have the good and the bad.

We know the founder or the fall guy for the Illuminati was Adam Weishaupt, who was born a Jew, he converted to Romanism and became a priest, a Jesuit-trained professor of canon law, no less.

You have heard some of the vows that they have taken. Did he really leave the Order? You tell me. Did he fight against his church to build it up? Everyone needs an enemy.

As the story goes, he taught at Engelstock University. On the behest of the House of Rothschild, he defected and organized the Illuminati. But later he returned to Romanism, just before his death, surprising?

This tells me something. This was the last act of his life. Was his whole heart really into it, or did he merely follow orders from his Superiors and create an opposition from without to carry out the Jesuit plans from within?

Please remember, by then the order of Pope Clement XIV had been instituted in all of Europe. Russia was the only country that did not obey the order to remove the Jesuits. They were not restored until 1814.

This happened in July 13, 1773. They needed some way of operating within the Roman Empire, so I believe they created a Secret Society.

It is said that in 1770 he revised and modernized the age-old Protocols of Zionism. It is said that he completed his work in May 1, 1776. May 1, is a high holiday for the Marxist, Wiccans, Witches and Satanist. He was a trained Jesuit, he was a hated Jew within the Church, and I believe, within the Order. He had something to prove.

This revised plan of his required the destruction of all existing governments and religions. That objective was to be reached by dividing the masses of people. Surprisingly, this is the same goal of the Jesuits, the Marxist, the Masons, and the Vatican.

That is one version of many that I have read. This helps the Romans and Protestant hate the Jews, who they feel killed Jesus. We all know that it was a Roman soldier under the orders of a Roman Governor that did the actual killing.

Therefore, the Gentiles murdered him. Of course, He was falsely accused by the Jews and placed on trial by them. For that, they are guilty.

Many will hate me for saying it, but that is the Bible. Nevertheless, the Gentiles were there; they had their say at the trial and carried out the order with Lust. Therefore, all of humankind is guilty of the murder of Christ.

Therefore, we see the foundations for the hate of the Jews, which Hitler carried to the next level. First, they preach hate, and then they act and commit murder.

Hitler carried this out as a good Roman; he fulfilled the desires of Rome. As True Christians, we must remember that our real enemy is not our brother or sister that we see with our natural eyes.

But our true enemy is the prince of the power of the air. You see, the Devil hates the Jew, the Gentile, the white man and the black man. He hates the young and he hates the old, and he loves to inject us with this hate.

The names of those who have ruled over others and enslaved them, who have plundered and destroyed many lives has changed, but that spirit that guides them has remained the same. He has turned brother against brother, husband against wife, and nation against nation.

The devil uses men as toys. They think that they are great and powerful, but they are hell bound. Many want to throw off true civilization and act as animals, to fulfill their lust upon their brother or sister.

The coming Squeeze with the coming wars will give them the excuse for the killing of one another. Moslem, Orthodox or Roman will all be put to the test when the climate for killing arises. In this last war, like in many others, the killing will be futile and meaningless.

It is said that the Rothschilds have financed every war beginning with the French Revolution, have they played double or triple agents? This is said to have been done under various fronts or different named organizations to cool the trail for any investigator.

In the United States, the Council on Foreign Relations, CFR, has been used to heavily influence, if not take over our government, our Business, and our Media. They have succeeded.

Now with this, the Jesuit is at the head of this new organization, it takes shape and its forces are put in place. But there was no fear of them, because no one knew of them.

Therefore, they must be found out. So an unveiling had to take place. A rider was struck by lightning; he was carrying the secret plans of the Conspiracy. Was this truly an act of God or was this whole scene an act and the documents a plant?

Only God knows. Either way, this put people in fear throughout the ages. Now, we had an enemy and it was an enemy that the Church had told us to hate all along. This had worked out perfectly. The enemy was a Jew.

Satan has injected hatred and poison into the hearts of people back to the days of Cain and Abel. Those that seek power and control for the sake of it and have no character are a curse upon humanity.

Many are ready and willing to throw off civilization and act likes animals. They do not understand that they will live in vain and die in their sins.

The only thing they will take with them from this earth is their sinful character. For when the times comes, they will follow their false messiah and will not inherit the Kingdom of God.

The Murder of Truth

"The Roman Pontiff...as supreme pastor and teacher of all the faithful." RCC Catechism #891, p. 256 (Source-www.jesus-is-lord.com)

Now let us cover this one more time but a little deeper. Throughout history, the Vatican has resorted to murder among other things to bring people, nations and tongues under her sway. But it was the murder of one of its own that has brought unwanted attention to the followers of the Pope.

Albino Luciani had embarked on a revolution within the Vatican. It was a dramatic reshuffle. He was to set the Church in new directions. His plan was to remove and strip six powerful men, all were Freemasons.

This new Pope had found that within the Vatican City State there was over 100 Masons, ranging from a Cardinal to priests. Canon Law stated that to be a Freeman ensured automatic excommunication. Luciani also found an illegal Masonic lodge, which had penetrated far beyond Italy in its search for wealth and power. It called itself P2. The fact that it had penetrated the Vatican walls and formed links with priests, bishops, and even cardinals made P2 anathema to Albino Luciani.

Over at least three of these men lurked the shadow of another, Licio Gelli. Men called him 'Il Burattinaio'-the Puppet Master. The puppets were many and were placed in numerous countries.

He controlled P2 and through it, he controlled Italy. Now it was time for the Puppet Master to strike back, in Buenos Aires, the city where he discussed the problem of the new Pope with Calvi.

The Puppet Master had chosen this place, I believe, because it was a stronghold for him. It was here that he had organized the triumphant return to power of General Peron. Peron subsequently kneeled at Gelli's feet.

They all knew that if Marcinkus, Sindona or Calvi were threatened by the action planned by Albino Luciani, it was time for Licio Gelli to remove that threat to his power.

It was abundantly clear that on September 28th, 1978, these six men, Marcinkus, Villot, Calvi, Sindona, Cody and Gelli had much to fear if the Papacy of John Paul I continued.

It is equally clear that all of them stood to gain in a variety of ways if Pope John I should suddenly die. He did. One of those six men had, by early evening of September 28th, 1978, already initiated a course of action to resolve the problems that Albino Luciani's Papacy was posing.

One of these men was at the very heart of a conspiracy that applied a uniquely Italian solution. So if they are not above killing and controlling their own, what about you and me. This again reminds me of the assassination of JFK; many of the men that JFK removed form power led the investigation into his assassination. That makes all the sense to me. (Source-In God's Name: An Investigation into the Murder of Pope John Paul I, by David A. Yallop.)

Their history

"For the Roman Pontiff, by reason of his office as Vicar of Christ, and as pastor of the entire Church has full, supreme, and universal power over the whole Church, a power which he can always exercise unhindered." RCC Catechism # 882, p.254 (source-www.jesus-is-lord.com)

After the Napoleonic wars, it seems that the Elite of the world and the Illuminati assumed that all nations were so destitute and so weary of wars that they would be glad to receive any solution for world peace.

So they set up the Congress of Vienna in 1814-15 and tried to create the first League of Nations. But Alexander, Czar of Russia caught them in the act and resisted and it fell apart. He was now a sworn enemy and Russia and the Eastern Catholic Church had to be dealt with. Let us look at some history.

I am sure that evil men inspired by Satan have conspired to control portions of history and that they have planned events and that those events have taken place.

Sometimes, these events must have seemed to have worked out perfectly. Then at other times, they have lost complete control of those events.

It was as if there was an invisible hidden force working against them. And maybe it was, may be it was God. For we all know that God uses men to carry out His plans also.

Now as a Christian, we know that everything works for the good of those that love and serve the Lord. So whatever happens or whatever may come our way, God has prepared a plan for us.

But as far as man is concerned, these things do happen as an accident, there are coincidences, and there are happenstances. Neither man nor Satan controls every event that happens on the earth.

They may try and use those events afterward, but they do not and will not ever control everything. God does, and He always will. This is their pyramid of power.

```
                    Lucifer
                      /\
                    Rome
                   /     \
            Jesuits  Illuminati
               /            \
          Religions      Humanists
             /                \
    Roman Churches      Communist/Socialist
          /                      \
Non-/Denominations (All)   Political Parties (All)
    _____
```

The New Religious, Political, Economic World Order!

Six

Population Control

After 9-11, they came for the Muslims and Illegal combatants, and we did not speak up. One day, they will be coming for the Guns, the Home schoolers; the Homosexuals, the Christian Fundamentalist, the Protestant Evangelicals, the Romans, the Jews, the Blacks, the Poor, and lastly they will come for the Prostate nominal Church member. And there will be no one to help you.

Their greatest weapon is your fears and your hatred. For we fear much and we hate many. We think very highly of ourselves here in America, but we no longer meet the requirement as a great-civilized nation. These requirements are clearly stated in scripture and spoken of throughout history by great men and women.

But we as a nation and people must go on with what we do. We must pretend that we are still a nation with moral character and courage that is satisfactory to both God and man. And truly, we are only pretending, the lights have gone out, we are in gross darkness. Our greatness came from our families, the quality of our education, religious freedom, personal accountability and a small government.

In the home, the father and mothers exercised discipline in the up-bringing of their children. The parents, not the government took responsibility for the child's education, and a religious education was part of that home.

But we began to get away from the laws of God. The television of the 50s helped bring in the hippies of the 60s; the government, namely the CIA, began flooding the streets with LSD to see how it would affect the sub culture. It now is its mainstream. Other gods began to rise up in our lives, money, power, prestige, sex, and worldly pleasures. Now we worship them every day.

It has taken a disaster to bring out the real heroes in America, the common man. Many are calling for a Religious and Social revival in the land. I have the words of a Prophet, it is too late for the nation, and it is time to get right with God as an individual. "Blessed is the nation whose God is the Lord, the people whom He has chosen as His heritage." PSALM 33:12

The Second Beast

"Those who manipulate this unseen mechanism of society constitute an invisible government which is the true ruling power of our country. Our minds are molded, our tastes are formed, our ideas suggested, largely by men we have never heard of." Walter Bernays, Propaganda-1928

Since the time of Nimrod to today, man has been preparing for a One World Government. It started with an organization and religion called Mystery Babylon. Its seat of power has moved with the people across lands and seas. Until today, we have Rome. It is the beast that seats on seven hills; it is the head of the Ten Toed Monster. It is the spiritual guide and leading spirit of the U.N.

But now let us look back to the turn of the 20th Century when there was a call for a Global Government, this organization was called The League of Nations. It is now called the United Nations. The goal of this organization is to rule the world. The muscle of this organization is the United States of America. Through the power of this second beast, any nation or people be it large or small that does not abide by its rules must pay a great prices in lives and have the potential of losing their sovereignty as a nation. Perhaps Americans were too concerned about this powerful U.N. ruling other nations, when it was us that they needed to fear. But in time, it will be America that will feel the force of this power as it turns and rents her to pieces.

America, inspired by the Vatican and backed by the U.N. will enforce upon the world the dreadful "Mark of the Beast". The Prophet, William Branham made it very clear that in Revelation 13:1-17 this once Lamb Nation-America will begin to speak as a Dragon.

"And 'He' (USA) had power to give life unto the Image of the Beast(Rome), that the Image of the Beast (Rome)should both speak, and cause as many as would not worship the Image should be killed."

Our great nation now sits as one of the five most powerful rulers in the world; it sits in the U.N.'s Security Council. This nation, with that power will one day force all nations, peoples and tongues into a Union of Churches! And those outside this Global, Universal Church, will be persecuted, hunted down and killed.

The American Inquisition

The Roman Crusades was brought about with religious propaganda and a call for a Just War. The end result of this call to action turned into a series of military campaigns.

They were Holy Wars that were generally sanctioned by the Pope in Rome. Their aim was to recapture the Holy Land and Jerusalem from the Muslims. But the target of these Crusades moved from the Holy Land to southern France to Constantinople. Once the blood flows, no one is safe.

Now they were not without a cause. The Fatimid caliph of Cairo, al-Hakim bi-Amr Allah, destroyed the Church of the Holy Sepulchre in Jerusalem.

This, with later stories that came to the ears of those in the western nations fuel the invasion plots. That along with a warrior class of Knights with nothing to do but fight among them selves.

The Roman West was at odds with the Greek Orthodox Eastern churches in Constantinople. But due to the invasion of the Muslims, the Patriarch of the East called on the Pope of the West for help, this launched the First Crusade in 1095.

This set up the notion of justified violence against the enemies of the Church. In the past, the Catholic Church had used violence against the Arians.

Then came the Occitan Cathars, unbelievers, other heretics and even Roman believers. The Pope's personal enemies were also targets. The use of violence by the Pope was becoming easier and easier.

Through the use of armed warfare, the Pope envisioned a uniting of the Eastern Church with the Western Church once again. This would bring about the end of the Great Schism of 1054. And would give rise to the supremacy of the Pope of Rome.

One of the first victims of the Crusades was the Jews, "schismatic" Orthodox Catholics and the Eastern Church in Constantinople in 1204. You see, if you differ with the Church Order as they see it, you must die. They saw themselves as being attacked first and their Holy Lands being taken over by the Muslims. The war for the Middle East was now joined.

Torture and Conquest

President Bush has on more than one occasion assured the nation and therefore the world that "torture is never acceptable, nor do we hand over people to countries that do torture." (Time Magazine).

Like Clinton before him, President Bush had to lie, for they both were found doing something evil. When confronted with the truth, their true character showed.

What he did not tell his fellow countrymen was that he had allowed a program called "Extraordinary Rendition". This was a very secretive program for aggressive methods of persuasion, or to put it in laymen terms, torture. With his new power after 9/11, came great abuses of authority that still goes on today.

If you were termed an "illegal enemy combatant" you could be picked up anywhere in the world and taken to a foreign nation and tortured until you confessed and yes, you would confess, sooner, if not later.

America had allowed herself to be swayed into the Dark Side. The enemies of freedom knew that when fear was placed over the heads of the people, they would and could do almost anything and we did.

The War on Terror was their excuse, this gave them their New Paradigm Shift in Domestic and World affairs that they needed to accomplish their Plan. Do we have a foundation for the action that we are taking? Yes, let us look to the past to understand the future!

With wars, there comes conquests. And with the conquests comes captives. Throughout the ages, man has always sought answers to his questions and during the time of war, the answers to his questions seems the most critical.

Therefore, he will and does proceed with the notion that the end justifies the means. But man also seeks to control and convert heretics and unbelievers to his faith or to his way of life, and even to his way of living. And so we are today.

The Spanish did not create the Inquisition; a papal bull issued by Pope Lucius III to attack the Albigensian heresy created this. From this act came a number of tribunals.

Ferdinand and Isabella established the Spanish Inquisition in 1478. They established the Inquisition in their Kingdom to maintain Roman orthodoxy. This was not abolished until 1834. Freedom of religion did not exist in Spain or any of its territories. Now you should be thankful for living in America even more.

Their goal was to establish and maintain a religious and political unity. Their aim also was for a centralized government. In this move, they were going after the political and religious opposition, they wanted to weaken it, if not destroy it. They focused on the powerful yet minority group of Jewish converts some had arisen to high places of power in the kingdom.

This was a Political, Religious and Economic Inquisition. For one of their measures was the confiscation of the property of their victims. This was also the goal of those in the time of Esther.

So we can see in this Tribulation that even if you were to convert to the false religion in the coming world order, you would still be hunted down and killed as were these Jews. If you will not convert, you will die and if you convert, you will die a fool.

Like the anti-gun lobby of today, back then we had the anti-book lobby. They produced an index of prohibited books. Today, every book you buy or sell or borrow from the library will be listed under your name. They know you and they know what you are reading.

These books were burnt. This included a Bible that you could read in your own language, for knowledge is power and the ignorant is a powerful tool in the hands of a tyrant. Back then, you had to have a license to print, a license to read and possess a book.

This will be the cast once again. As the Communist ran Russia with terror, the Inquisitors ran Spain. Death came to people for simply speaking their minds.

As it is today in America, you can be arrested, jailed and held without legal council. This is done without knowledge of your family.

In fact, they could be arrested and jailed if they spoke out about your arrest. Like the Inquisition, America has set up laws and instruction for torture.

The tribunals consisted of two inquisitors, a calificador and alguacil (bailiff) and a fiscal (prosecutor). There was no Defense Attorney, as it is in the American Inquisition; you are on your own.

As it is in the drug war in America, what is confiscated is turned over to the Police. This drives up the confiscation of Vehicles, property and Money.

This was done in the Spanish Inquisition, and it works. The rich make good heretics or good martyrs; it all depends on how you look at it.

Fear of the torture produced many false witnesses against their neighbors, so it has proven with our own Inquisition. For those that are tortured will talk, for they are only human, but they will say whatever they think their torturer wants them to say to get them to stop, if it is only for a while.

The accusations were anonymous and the defendant would never face his accuser in court. For envy or even personal resentment, you could end up standing before the Inquisitors.

That old aunt or uncle that you never liked, or even sister against brother. The lies kept following without much if any evidence against them.

Preventative Action

They felt they had to act, and act fast. Therefore they would detain someone before they could act and cause harm. Some defendants wee held for lengthy incarceration of up to two years before they were brought before the court.

His property was taken and used to pay for the trial and the accuser's living expenses. His family was left out and to suffer. This was done with the utmost secrecy. They were isolated and cut off from the world. Some would die in prison, never knowing why they had been jailed. Finally, when the accused was brought before the tribunal, he was given council, but that council was limited.

A Global Papa

The Office of the Pope of Rome has been accepted by most of the world as its spiritual leader and moral guide. Through the

Ecumenical Movement that came about through the Vatican II Council, great men in the Protestant Faith, even here in America, have called Pope the "The Moral Leader of the West."

We see these things unfold before our eyes, and knowing that the time of the End is at hand. We watch these spiritual leaders spreading their politized Gospel to their people as they try and control this American government through the voting booths and daily polls.

As we see our President marching off to war, first in this country, then in that country, we can see how our nation is exercising all the power of the First Beast, Rome. The goal of Rome is to rule the world; it will do it through America!

Rome and Protestant America are together again, Rome is the Master and America is her servant. The true believers in America will have to make a stand and when we do, we will be cut out of this fellowship altogether.

It will start slowly at first and then it will grow. And then it will lead to a press or a Squeeze and we will be pressed out for a trial. This is why I am writing this book now. This book is for all that read it, but I am sending it out to the total lost and not for the Bride of Christ, but to the Church.

We know that the Squeeze, the Third Pull, the Bride Revival, and the Mark of the Beast are all tied together. We know that they will be happening at the same time.

We know that during the time of the Squeeze, the Church and State will come together and will be forcing its beliefs on others, it is at this time that God will manifest His power, God will come on the scene and make known His power and presence, but not to all. This will be a work of the spirit.

Soon, church doors will be closed and our suffering will begin. But be not afraid, this is not meant to destroy us. But know that we must be refined and our character tested. This will help to purify us and make us ready.

The Bride and the nominal church have been waiting for a revival. Some became discouraged because it seemed to take too long. Some have been calling for miracles and signs and wonders

Not realizing that it will take the SQUEEZE before we can manifest God's signs and wonders to the fullness. God pressured Israel time and time again to return to her homeland. He must now pressure us to return to our first Love, Jesus Christ.

Like Israel, we will have no hope but God. We will be forced from our homes into the wilderness of our own country, all for the cause of Christ. The planned persecution is coming soon.

In America, we now have the OFFICE OF RELIGIOUS PERSECUTION MONITORING or O.R.P.M. The President of the United States has appointed a national director. This director will be under the supervision of the Secretary of State, and will coordinate activity with the United Nations. These are some of the provisions set forth in the Law. I first saw this information on a web page by Brother C.W. Wood. Much of the background information here is from his article.

1. Study, rank and evaluate all religions.
2. Penalize churches that do not comply.
3. Approve or disapprove licenses for all ministers.
4. Establish national standards for acceptable religious practices.
5. Forbid financial contributions to churches not approved.
6. Seize bank accounts and property of those not approved.
7. Monitor newspapers, TV, Radio, Mail and Internet for violation of Hate Laws.
8. Target spiritually defective individuals who refuse their unity.
9. Work with government law enforcement agencies to see that religious Unity Laws are enforced, and that all churches and religious organizations are registered with O.R.P.M.

This law came from bill H.R. 2431. It was Congressman Frank Wolf and twenty-six other Congressmen that first signed this bill. It later made it though the Senate and became law. Congressman Wolf received his Law Degree from Georgetown University in 1965. This is a Jesuit University founded in 1789, the same year of the US Constitution.

America's Blowback

Americans refuse to look into the mirror and see the evil that America has done across this world. Millions of Americans have no idea; they cannot find the answer, the reason why, why so many people in the world hate Americans.

But we all know that America has dropped guided missiles and bombs all over the planet, but still she wonders why these people should want to throw them back at her.

In the beginning of this New Millennium, we needed a war to continue the American Way across the globe, we chose Iraq. In the Bush administration, Dick Cheney was the muscle man. He leaned on the CIA and its analysts to produce the intelligence that the administration wanted to hear.

But this is not the first time and it will not be the last time for this administration or for a future administration. For those in power know what they want to hear, and they will take a lie just as quick as the truth, to justify their actions.

Bush clones took over the CIA. They are seeking the same objective, more power and more control, in the world and in America. The CIA has been and is a servile arm of the secret government that it helped create. The true Americans still working in the agency can see the dangers clearly. But what can they do or what can they say, nothing. Well, they leak information when they can.

The Bush administration created the Office of Special Plans in the Pentagon, its purpose was to search for information on

Iraq's hostile intention against the US and its links to terrorists. All the while, the CIA was suppressing 911 information.

With 911, the CIA has expanded into a monster, with it secret army at the complete control of the administration. Congress and the judicial system has lost control of this massive secret death and torture machine. But most Americans are more than happy with the outcome. All the while, the secrecy of this administration increases day by day.

A great deal of Americans feel that we have the right to torture our non-combatant, non-prisoner guests. But let the same thing happen to an American, oh how sad we get.

If you care about America and your future, you should read the book Blowback by Chalmers Johnson. This book was written before 9/11. His most recent book is the Sorrows of Empire. Next, I would recommend to you Ghost Wars by Steve Coll. We must take the time and look inward as well as out for the real evil in the world today.

The time for the turn to the Right

So what are we waiting for? The laws are already on the books to enslave us. They are waiting for the right timing to put them in action.

The Enforcement Agencies have grown, after 9/11, they are even more established. Though the Patriot Act and other laws, we will be feeling the effect soon enough.

The Federal Government no longer has to abide by any laws or rules, as a declared enemy of the state, as so ordered by the Attorney General, you would become a non-person. We must adhere to and abide by all orders sent down to us from the mighty Federal Government.

This truly is a wilderness. First, they have started the fear of the terrorist, then the fear of our government, then starts the government using our fears. How soon will you feel it, the

Persecution from this government, it once was Lamb, but now it is as a Dragon.

The government says that it established this law and organization to protect us from dangerous and radical religious sects and cults. But in this government lies the biggest and most dangerous sects and cults in the world, Masons and the Skull and Bones. Now this law came in under Clinton, who is said to be a witch, along with his wife. Now who truly needs protection?

This helps and fosters the mainline denominational church system, for now, but in the end, they too will fall. Soon you will be called on to join a church that belongs to the World Church order, what will you do, this is the age when you will be forced to join the United World Religion.

This is the age of the global church. President Bush consulting his Bishops and Cardinal. The Vatican knows to control world politics; they have to control Washington and New York. The Vatican has over 1 billion members worldwide. It controls those who control the world finances.

When the day comes and you do not belong to the World Church, you will not be able to buy or sell. You will have nothing. Many will think that they will be able to serve God from within the Anti-Christ System and its Hierarchy. The people of America and the world will follow these false Shepherds right into serving Lucifer, and then they will be led to the slaughter. Yes, there is a Squeeze and there are many AFFLICTIONS that are heading our way, but in Christ Jesus, we will prevail.

Hoses 5:15 **"I will go and return to my place till they acknowledge their offense and seek my face. In their AFFLICTION they will seek me early."**

You will have to get off that fence this time. Some people will stay with Christ; others will stray towards the World Church. This stand will cost you everything. It will not be easy.

The Patriot Act

The expansion of the power of the Federal Government had been growing for years. But after September 11, 2001, overnight there were revisions of the nation's surveillance, laws begin to take effect. The nation began to spy upon its own citizens in new ways.

Or shall I say in a more public ways. Out went judicial oversight and public accountability. No longer would you be able to challenge the federal government searches in court.

Congress had long rejected this provisions. There would be little if any discussion or hearings about the Bills before them. Some Senators later complained that they had little chance to read the Bill before having to vote on it.

The propaganda machinery went into overdrive, and members of Congress were threatened to be blamed if they did not vote for the bill and another attack was to take place. They showed no rational reason for the bill, was it really our lack of domestic surveillance laws and their enforcement that allowed this attack. Or did someone have a hidden agenda?

Now the government conducts secret searches without any notice to the owner. It forces doctors, bookstores, universities and internet servers to turn over records on you.

This power will go on with out any oversight by anyone outside of the agency. Given this power, there will be abuses. There is no longer a need for a reasonable suspicion of the person. The Constitution is eroded and powerless. And the American people are more than happy.

Patriot Act II

It did not take long for the Imperial Forces to muster for another attack on our freedoms. For less than two years after Congress passed the USA Patriot Act, it came up with the Domestic Security Enhancement Act.

The first Act brought back the power of the CIA to spy and operate inside America. That Act had envisioned sweeping power for surveillance, wiretapping, detention and prosecution. The second Act allows the government to keep the identity of the detained in connection with a terror investigation. Until charges were filed, however long that would take.

The federal government would be allowed to conduct warrantless searches. It provided for wiretappings without court orders. The government would not have to release information about hazards posed by chemicals and plants.

Individuals engaged in civil disobedience could risk losing their citizenship. Lawful immigrants could be stripped of their rights to a fair hearing on their deportation, and a federal judge would not be able to review this immigration ruling. The abuses of power go on and on, and the American public thanked their new masters in Washington, we voted our freedoms away.

Seven

World Government

We are being brought together in segments. First the Europeans, now North America. Then Southeast Asia, then it moved to South America.

And one day you will see an American and European Commonwealth of nations. There is a grouping and regrouping of nations all the time.

The alignment of the Ten Horns and the Ten Toes of Bible prophecy is being fulfilled right before our eyes. And because we dare say it, we are called crazy.

Ask yourself what are you doing while the global development movement moves forward with its plans. They have their Economic initiatives, Political, Military, and Intelligence alignments.

They have their Unified Religious strategies that bring together the religious world through their Ecumenical, Interfaith worship services and interfaith celebrations. They are achieving their goals one person, one state, one nation at a time.

Nothing is too small and nothing is too big for them. They want it all and they need to have it all, to bring in the world that they desire to have.

But not all are falling into step with their global movement. Some Atheists, Buddhists, Muslims and Christians, are awakening and coming to realize that through this process, this movement will lead us to a Global Socialist-Capitalist Order and to a Global Occupation.

What are their plans, why are they aligning us and painting us into a corner? For once, they have targeted the sovereign Nation-states as their enemy, and they plan to destroy this system of government. They are the Elite, they are the ruling class, and they feel they have a better way.

From the time of the League of Nations until now, they have sought to limit and to replace the nation-states system with a supranational world body. These groups are small, highly concentrated and very powerful.

They guide and direct the adoption process at varying levels using distinct and separate forces. These forces are directing this movement into a very specific direction.

They are private interests with power on a global scale. From the days of Woodrow Wilson, to Franklin D. Roosevelt, Harry Truman and now George Bush Jr., each man has been pushed in a direction not his own and has led our country into global governance.

It may not seem like it, but we are headed for a 10 nation/regional Worldwide One-party system. The U.N. or something more powerful, will be the central command center. Then there will be regional offices for each area. This system and subsystem will form a network of powerful men and women. They will create Dukedoms with all its inherent problems.

In this creation, the rich will get richer. And the middle class will fade to black, then to nothingness. This is their goal to standardize our cultural values and our social norms.

They want to control all financial systems and to have the only true global war fighting system. But first, they are more than happy to have America fight their wars and place other nations under her feet. Until it is time to make the world hate us, and eventually, they to will turn on us.

They need America now to maintain the necessary social cohesion of its own masses. This will be done through the permanent war footing. We are in the 100-year war. In this war, you cannot say anything against the establishment. If you do, you will be called a Traitor. They have real and/or imagined enemies that we are told to fear each day.

This is our fight and our country, can you imagine a global power and a global leader acting like George Bush, wait until we speak out against the world government under the New World Order. It will be death.

We no longer have the authority, this is no longer of the people and by the people, we have the number, but that is useless, we are powerless. They form the real power; they are the Elites, they are not subject to the democratic process, they will not bow down to an oversight community of any governmental body.

From the Seven Hills of Rome sits the Vatican, they send out the order, it travels to London, then across the seas to New York and finally the order reaches Washington.

The world is supervised from the Vatican. Its old power is returning to it day by day. Its political reach has been expanding for years. It has goals and it will achieve its goals. It maneuvers off and on stage to carry out it strategies that span the globe. It is truly a power to hold Washington in check.

The Visible Government

Our form of government has a short life span. A President only has 8 years to hold onto his power. The last Pope lasted 26 years. Our government is based in Washington D.C. Our city is not that old and its people are naïve to world plays. Rome has been there for thousands of years and it has been on the world stage several times. And its people are truly global. Its power and place on the world stage is unparallel.

Our national, State and Local governments are run by many of Rome's operatives. And the Vatican has placed undue pressure on the office holder during election years. What will we see in the coming midterm election in 2006? More pressure? Time will tell.

The Media

The media is a powerful governing body in our country. With it comes a powerful mass psychological warfare machine. They are a real power unto themselves. And they answer to the invisible hands that plan out the actions of the major visible players.

I see the move to get the American people to receive the dream of the Elite. The New World Order. At first, it was not received well; the people have been warned over and over again. But given time, the Elite knows how to play the Mob.

Right now, the Mob is nervous, suspicious and afraid. So the Elite has changed the name of the noose; they now call it-Globalization.

This is only a new name, the purpose has not changed. They still seek a World Government.

America is on the move with its Global imperialism. This move is far reaching and it has a religious side that most miss. Our place in the play will be over before long and then the center of the play will move to Europe. It is there the power and leadership will be headquartered.

This is spoken of in the book of Revelation. The reach of Americans is strong. The CIA and the NSA have gone into fellowship with every major group and every government on the face of the planet at one time. From the American Mafia to the Japanese Mafia, and Russian Mafia. Many people hear that and think they have the answer. The answer is more than what you can find in America. You have to go beyond that.

America will be and is playing a part in the grouping together of the 10 regional powers. But you cannot stop there. Look at the New Age Movement and how it is bringing into America and other western countries the Eastern Religions and their leaders. And see how they have brought their culture into the West, until now, the once great Christian nations and their people are too corrupt and too far-gone to turn back to God and His faith.

America is as Israel was before the Babylonians destroyed it. And so it will be with us. First, the Mystery Babylonians brought in their corrupt religion, causing God to turn his back on us. Then they will come in and raze us to the ground.

The Players
Who are they?

"You see, if you amount to anything in Washington these days, it is because you have been plucked or handpicked from an Ivy League school-Harvard, Yale, Kennedy School of Government-you've shown an aptitude to be a good Ivy League type, and so you're plucked so-to-speak, and you are assigned success. You are assigned a certain role in government somewhere, and then your success is monitored and tracked, and you go where the pluckers and the handpickers can put you." Rush Limbaugh February 7, 1995

They are men and women of renown in Europe, Asia and America. They come from the political and financial side. This makes up the Trilateral Commission. The American Globalist controls about 80% of the US economy. They live and breathe in the global financial Institutions, there they guide and steer the world of finance.

Their First Strike was Global Finance. Here they are moving the fastest. They have brought the many global currencies down to only two major global currencies-the US Dollar and the Euro. Soon it will be one global currency. That may be the Euro. But they will not stop there.

They will then move to electronic funds, some type of a credit and/or debit system. The card and/or later the tattoo will have the embedded chips. This is essential; there must be a centralized global –monitoring program. They are world controllers.

85

They are moving in steps and getting it done. The arrival of the One World Government will not be long. They have men like Robert Muller. He is involved with several global agencies and agendas. He is a professing Catholic who has served as a top UN political and spiritual advisor for the last three decades.

He is referred to as the UN's Prophet of Hope! Muller is working with Jay Gary an evangelical Christian and a community leader. He runs a BEGIN program or Bi-millennial Global Interaction Network. There, he promotes interfaith and ecumenical groups and organizations.

Now many believe at some point we shall see the controlled collapse of the global financial infrastructure. Groups like the CFR may be planning this. They have been carefully planned this through their Financial Vulnerabilities Project and New International Financial Architecture programs. In the days of Joseph, the people sold themselves into slavery rather than starve. So it will be in the days of the world's financial collapses.

Some of the groups involved in the move to world socialism are large, some are small, some are regional and some are global. Here we will look at two groups that show us a vast different in appearance and operations. But they are lead to the same goal a new world order, let us take a look.

The Groups
The Fabian Society

They get their name from a Roman general by the name of Quintus Fabius Maximus. It is a British socialist intellectual movement with sister societies in Australia, New Zealand, and Canada.

Their cause is socialism, by reform rather then arms. It is the foundation for the British Labour Party.

It was founded on 4 January 1884 in London. Many noted intellectuals of that day flowed into the society. Many of the members seemed to admire the Soviet Union.

They were against tenants paying rent and wanted to nationalize the land. Its most famous member today is Tony Blair.

The Club of Rome

This is another global think tank. On its web site, it states that it is: "a group of scientist, economists, businessmen, international high civil servants, and heads of state and former heads of State who poll together their different experiences from a wide range of backgrounds to come to a deeper understanding of the world problematique." It is composed of active members, associate members, honorary members and institutional members.

Its reach is into international politics. It was founded in 1968. The Club published a report on "The Limits of Growth" in 1972 and sold 30 million copies. This group started out with a reported inner circle of six members. Its founders were an Italian scholar and industrialist named Aurelio Peccei and Alexander King, a Scottish scientist. It is a club of elites and some call it a Neo-Malthusianism organization.

First, let us look at Malthusianism- this style of doctrine came about during the industrial revolution, it is a capitalist idea, with political and economic implication. This idea brought about the Poor Law Amendment Act of 1834 in England, which opponents indicated would force the poor to emigrate, or to work for lower wages. It can be seen in the theories of Charles Darwin.

This doctrine came from Thomas Malthus, his concept spoke of how limited resources would keep populations in check and that it would reduce economic growth. Those who follow this concept advocate the use of contraceptives. Hence, the population control stands in the Club of Rome.

The Bilderberg Group

You can only get in by invitation. And you would be one out of about 130 guests. And they are the Elite of the political, business, media, and academia world. This is not an open or public event. But it is an annual, secretive and exclusive club or group. They meet in Europe, the US and Canada. Its first meeting took place in the Hotel de Bilderberg. This is in Oosterbeek, near Arnhem in the Netherlands. The year was 1954.

The Orange Order

This is a large Protestant secret society, which has many mysterious esoteric rituals, secret degrees and practices. This is a global order with ten of thousands of members in Ireland, Britain, America, Australia, Canada, and New Zealand.

This Order was founded on 21 September 1795 by three well-known Freemasons, two of which were local pub owners. This band of brothers was formed after a fight with the Catholic on one of the founder's land; his building was burnt to the ground.

A former Orangemen have written a book about the lodge; Paul Malcomson called "Behind Closed Doors." There is a good web site called Evangelical Truth that covers this group.

"There is...an inner core of intimate associates who unquestionably knew that they were members of a group devoted to a common purpose and outer circle of large number on whom the inner circle acted by personal persuasion, patronage distribution, and social pressure. It is probable that most members of the outer circle were not conscious that they were being used by a secret society." Carroll Quigley-The Anglo-America Establishment

The Council on Foreign Relation (CFR) and the Trilateral Commission have been in control of America for some time. The rich and the powerful founded them both. Colonel Edward Mandell House founded The Council on Foreign Relations in

1921. He had been the chief advisor and alter ego (other self) of President Woodrow Wilson. Wilson once said of House that their minds were one. House lived in the White House with President Wilson for some time.

He held sway in the Wilson Administration and he was the most powerful man in this Administration from 1913 to 1921. He was a Marxist. His goals were to socialize the United States.

In 1921, House wrote the book "Philip Dru Administrator". In this book, he stated that he was working for "Socialism as dreamed of by Karl Marx." He hated the Constitution and it seems everything that America stands for.

In this book, House's main character sets himself up as a Dictator. In this book, we see the conquest of America and the destruction of the American way. Phillip Dru controls America and uses his power to create a socialist government. House loved it.

As we look back over Wilson's administration, we see the House book being lived out. For in his book he called for the establishment of a state-controlled central bank.

And in 1913, during the House-dominated Wilson Administration, this had been proposed. And it was House that set up the Federal Reserve Act for Wilson.

This Act gave us a private central bank. This bank now had the power to create the money of the United Sates. This Act had removed this power away from the United States Congress.

Then came the 16th Amendment to the United States Constitution. This gave us the graduated income tax. This was another proposal by Karl Marx.

So it seems that Colonel House's purpose from the start was to destroy the freedoms and independence of the United States. And it seems that his goal was to lead this country into a Global government.

The CFR organization at once began to attract men of power and influence. Then came the financing from the Rockefeller Foundation and the Carnegie Foundation. In the FDR years,

CFR members gained domination over the State Department. They have maintained their control ever since.

The Present Breed

Now it comes to our day. And we have the current crop of Jesuit trained and secret society sponsored souls roaming the land. Their rise to power will forever go unchecked.

They will control the Presidency, the Cabinet, the State Department, the Senate, the House, the CIA and the NSA. They will control the whole house of cards. Then you truly will see a different Beast in America.

Carroll Quigley, the mentor of President Clinton, was a Professor of History at Georgetown, a Jesuit University, and he was a member of the CFR. He wrote several books. Here are some statements from a few of those books.

The Anglo-American Establishment

"The Rhodes Scholarships, established by terms of Cecil Rhodes' seventh will, are known to everyone. What is not known is that Rhodes in five previous wills left his fortune to form a secret society, which was to devote itself to the preservation and expansion of the British Empire. And what does not seem to be known to anyone is that this secret society was created by Rhodes and his principal trustee, Lord Milner, and continues to exist to this day."

"**In the middle of 1890s Rhodes had a personal income of at least a million pounds sterling a year (then worth about US $5,000,000) which was spent so freely for his mysterious purpose that he was usually overdrawn on his account. ...these purposes centered on his desire to federate the English-speaking people and to bring all the habitable portions of the world under their controls. For this purpose Rhodes left part of his great fortune to found the Rhodes Scholarships at Oxford...the power and influence of the**

Rhodes-Milner group in British imperial affairs and in foreign policy since 1889, although not widely recognized, can hardly be exaggerated...the American branch of this English Establishment extended much of its influence through five American newspapers..."

"Tragedy & Hope":

"There does exist, and has existed for a generation, an international Anglophile network which operates, to some extent, in the way the radical Right believes the Communist act. In fact, this network, which we may identify as the Round Table Groups, has no aversion to cooperating with the Communist, or any other groups, and frequently does so. I know of the operations of this network because I have studied it for twenty years and was permitted for two years, in the early 1960s, to examine its papers and secret records.

"The CFR is the American Branch of a society which originated in England, and which belies that national boundaries should be obliterated, and a one-world rule established."

Here was a man that traveled in the inner circles of the establishment. A Philosopher and teacher to one of our Presidents. A rapid and acute reader. He had an exceptional range of knowledge on many fields.

Did he lie to us about what he had seen and heard? Was he insane like some would like you to believe? This would discredit all that he had to say, and that is what they want. He wrote Tragedy and Hope in 1966, Evolution of Civilizations in 1979 and The Anglo-American Establishment in 1981. You do the research and you tell me.

This man worked as a lecturer and it was said that his lectures were spellbinding. He served as a consultant to the U.S. Department of Defense, the U.S. Navy, the Smithsonian Institute, and the House Select Committee on Astronautics and

Space Exploration. Search him out and you decide. Was it the truth or was it a lie? Now let us move to other witnesses.

"I claim...the existence of a conspiracy for the destruction of the Western World as the prelude for shepherding mankind into a sheep's pen run as a prelude to One World tyranny." A.K. Chesterton-The New Unhappy Lords: An Exposure of Power Politics.

"The most powerful clique in these elitist groups have one objective in common-they want to bring about the surrender of the sovereignty of the national independence of the United States. A second clique of international members in the CFR comprises the Wall Street international bankers and their key agents. Primarily, they want the world banking monopoly from whatever power ends up in control of global government." Rear Admiral Chester Ward-member of CFR for 16 years

"The ultimate aim of the CFR is to create a one-world socialist system, and to make the U.S. an official part of it." Dan Smoot, former FBI Agent

I could show some of you a great deal of proof, but you are like the founder of the Jesuits, Ignatius, he once said:

"I will believe that the white that I see is black if the hierarchical Church so defines it."

So tell me what is your absolute in your life, or do you not have one? What do you rally to in the time of trials and testing? Is it God or is it man?

Is it carnal or is it spiritual? The action of these groups and people are treasonous. And you may belong to some of these groups, do they really have your best interest at hand.

They have stated that their goals are to put the United States of America under the power of a global government, and to take away your freedoms, are your eyes open yet?

Thomas Dewy, a CFR member, was the Republican candidate in 1944 and in 1948. They have been moving to control the political parties for sometime. They knew that if they could, they would control who would be President.

Their influence came in as early as Andrew Jackson, and as recently as Eisenhower and Nixon. They both were members of the CFR. Their reach was far, it reached into the likes of Stevenson, Kennedy, Humphrey and McGovern, all CFR members. President Kennedy upset many players on the American and World stage. From the Mafia, Vatican to the Military, many felt betrayed by him. He was making moves that had to be stopped.

The American people finally saw that they had been set up in an election year; the stage was set in Florida. This was not the first time. Kennedy had his Chicago. But even when their vote counts, they are electing CFR members or someone trained by a Jesuit. Their influence reaches into all areas of American life.

"Does it not seem strange to you that these men just happen to be CFR and just happen to be on the Board of Governors of the Federal Reserve, that absolutely controls the money and interest rates of this great country without benefit of Congress? A privately owned organization, the Federal Reserve, which has absolutely nothing to do with the United States of America!" Barry Goldwater-With No Apologies

"Not every member of the CFR is fully committed to carrying out Edward Mandell House's conspiratorial plan. Many have been flattered by an invitation to join a study group, which is what the CFR calls itself. Others go because of personal benefit, such as a nice job and a new importance. But all are used to promote the destruction of U.S. sovereignty." Jack Newell

Members of the CFR cover every aspect of the American life. Those members are under an oath and a code of silence, on what is said and done in the CFR meetings.

"The CFR, dedicated to one-world government, financed by a number of the largest tax-exempt foundations, and welding such power and influence over lives in the areas of finance, business, labor, military, education, mass communication-media, should be familiar to every American concerned with good government, and with preserving and defending the

U.S. Constitution and our free-enterprise system. Yet, the nation's right-to-know machinery, the news media, usually so aggressive in exposures to inform our people, remain conspicuously silent when it comes to the CFR, it members and their activates. The CFR is the establishment. Not only does it have influence and power in key decision-making positions at the highest levels of government to apply pressure from above, but it also finances and use individuals and groups to bring pressure from below, to justify the high level decisions for converting the U.S. from a sovereign Constitution Republic into a servile member of a one-world dictatorship." Congressman John R. Patrick

You may as well keep your blinders on. It is too late for your body anyway. But you still have time for your soul. That is until God shuts the door. Do not believe the story that as long as you have breathe in your body, you have a chance. There were many dead men walking and talking to Christ in His day and so it is in ours. Some of you belong to the Total Lost, you have eyes, but you cannot see, you have ears, but you cannot hear. Pharaoh and his son were dead men long before Moses left Egypt, for they were spiritually dead, stand up against Moses and the True God.

Trilateral Commission

The Rockefellers financed the CFR and gave them the building were they meet. But this country and this world needed a different angle for the attack, so to complete the encirclement, they created another monster.

This monster was cloned in 1973. It was named The Trilateral Commission. It has the same goal: a Global Government.

The mastermind behind this organization was Zbigniew Brzezinski. In his book "Between Two Ages", he praised Marxism, just as Mandel House once did, he spoke of the United States as being obsolete, as did Mandel House. He praised the formation of a one-world government.

And like Edward Mandell House, he had a President to teach and to lead about. He stated:

"Marxism is simultaneously a victory of the external, active man over the inner, passive man and a victory of reason over belief."

"Marxism disseminated on popular level in the form of Communism, represented a major advance in man's ability to conceptualize his relationship to his world."

"Marxism supplied the best available insight into contemporary reality."

Backed financially by the Rockefellers, the organization brought together North America, Western Europe, and Japan. They were now linked and locked into an economic, political and defense relationship, this was at a level never before obtained. This became their forum to reach out to the developing and to the Communist countries.

Zbigniew Brzezinski became the Director of this beast. Jimmy Carter was now a student of Brzezinski, and he became a founding member of the Commission.

Over 284 CFR and Trilateral Commission members populated Jimmy Carter's Administration. This brought the collapse of the American Republic and the overthrow of the U.S. Constitution. We did not make it to our 200th birthday free and clear.

President Reagan replaced Carter and was forced to take in George Bush Sr., a Skull and Bones member. Reagan was controlled to the fullest extent. He barely knew what was going on in his Administration.

You can now see the effect of The Council on Foreign Relation and The Trilateral Commission on the affairs of our nation. The President continually calls for action by the U.N., this will continue until one day they will act. And when this Beast acts, it will act in a most powerful way. America will then have to step aside and step in line with this world body. This is their goal.

America does not act in its own interest. We fight wars for the good of the global community and not America. And these wars we do not win.

We tie ourselves to international agreements, pacts, and conventions that do not meet the needs or the desires of the American people. Our Federal, State and Local leaders are push to adapted a worldview. Socialism is preached the world over and never more so now in America.

The Communist States have become our partners in the alliance leading this world government. This was worked out in their plans. Now comes the merging of the nation-states into the image of the socialist-capitalist state. Russia has done its part and we must do ours. Their goal seems to be to met somewhere in the middle.

"The Trilateral Commission is international, and it is intended to be the vehicle for multinational consolidation of the commercial and banking interests by seizing control of the political government of the United States. The Trilateral Commission represents a skillful, coordinated effort to seize control and consolidate the four centers of power-political, monetary, intellectual, and ecclesiastical." Barry Goldwater

It does not matter if they belong to the Jesuits, Freemasons, CFR, Trilateral Commission or the various other groups. They are not all in the know, nor are they committed to the overthrow and destruction of the United States.

Most are just Pawns and their activity and loyalty forms a cover for those that truly desire America to fall. It is not the many, but the few that are in the know and in control.

Some come for the fortune and others for the fame. Some come for the lifestyle. It does not matter, God called all Baal worshippers to Repent, so it is today. It does not matter if you are Catholic or Methodist; it does not matter if you follow the teaching or live the life that their faith calls for.

You are still counted and numbered among them. The same is for the members of these groups. If they are in these groups and do not know what is happening, then their eyes are covered over and they are blind. God calls us to the light. Look around, do a little more research. Do not just think only of yourself.

America, you are not free, and this is not a free country. Just speak out against the war and you will see. Others foolishly think that by starting a Rebellion, they will overthrow the powerful Elites. You will only die and most likely in your sins. Then you will have to stand before an angry God.

You are both wrong. There are those that have sold their souls for the glory of Lucifer. They have enslaved the nations with their International Financial systems. Our hope lies in the hands of God.

Knights Hospitaller

This order is also called or known as Knights of Rhodes, Knights of Malta, it is a Paramilitary Catholic Organization, and CIA director William J. Casey was a member. It is also called the Cavaliers of Malta and the Order of St. John of Jerusalem.

This order was founded in Jerusalem after the First Crusades, sometime around 1100 A.D. It began as a Benedictine religious order, but became a Catholic military order, with its duty being to provide armed escorts to pilgrims traveling to the Holy Land.

It was later located on the Island of Rhodes due to the loss of the Holy Land, and then it moved again to Malta. The Sovereign Military Hospitaller Order of St. John of Jerusalem of Rhodes and of Malta or SMOM is one of its successors.

This Catholic Order has two headquarters, both in Rome. It claims national sovereignty and has been granted permanent observer status at the United Nations. It claims to be a sovereign entity other than a state.

So far, it has not been granted status as a non-member state by the U.N., but its status is as an entity and intergovernmental organization with an invitation to participate as an observer. It does have ambassadorial status with many nations and has diplomatic status with over 90 nations.

Eight

Rule by Secrecy

"The key to Rockefeller and Brzezinski's plan was to gain control of the executive branch of the U.S. government. The first step was the selection in 1973 of an ambitious, capable presidential candidate."
Craig Karpel

Switzerland was the last holdout from the New League of Nations. Now she has joined the family. Now all the nations of the world are joined to a single global political organization. Now with the nations aligning together, now with the environment and the global warming as their collective mind focus.

Now with the America superpower alienating the world against her, now with the U.N. amassing and accumulating great power and strength from its member states.

The call will soon go out for all nations to lay down their differences and unite as one, this call will be answered. How soon, I do not know, but one day this call will see its work done in the name of global peace and security. All nations will one day get together and work as one.

Why has America, which has the most freedoms, the most power, set herself to sell her soul to another, why? Because they do not and they will not serve the same God as we do. They want the United Nations power and its reach to grow.

They want the international treaty, which gives the UN unequal power on the global scene to be ratified in the U.S. Congress. They want the proposals to set up the UN as the major political and military authority in the new world government.

They have financed this great movement with old money and new money. The Rothschilds, to the Rockefellers, who then turn around and established finance trusts and think tanks.

How did it all start?

"I don't care who the government is, let me control the money and I will control the country." Rothschilds

For over 200 years in America there has been a coordinated, effective and irresistible force working to take over this country and its government. God had set this nation apart from all the other nations and gave it the most rights, freedoms and power than any other nation before it. But like Biblical Israel, we have become lazy, corrupt, and backslidden as a nation, and we will be punished, we will pay.

In 1919, a small group of influential bankers, lawyers, politicians and academics, who had earlier taken part in the Paris peace conference, met in the Parisian Hotel Majestic and reached agreement, they would form a group, a think tank that would design a New World Order.

Here was the creation of the Royal Institute of International Affairs (RIIA) in England. In America, its little sister would be christened the Council on Foreign Relations (CFR). Their goal: the gradual surrender of American suzerainty and the slow imposing of a socialist order on the population.

They have been after the wealth of middle class for some time. Because of the New Deal, socialism was brought into America, and has never left. As it was in Joseph's Egypt, man is just one disaster away from slavery.

This God-given wealth that we have has had an insulation effect and it has been a protection for you, your family and your rights. This is what has kept you from the will of the state.

Look to other less blessed countries and see how they are treated. Look at Russia and other countries that cannot pay their civil servants what we can pay ours. Yes, we do have corruption, but it is not because they are starving, but it is because of greed. That just shows the moral character of the man.

Our private funds, our private wealth empowers us and gives us a way to resist the evils that man would and could do, if we were poor and beggarly. Go to Thailand, the Philippines and Mexico and see how the rich nations and the sinful tourists prey upon the poor beggarly natives.

Or take a ride into your own back yard and see how, with out the gospel of Jesus Christ, people will allow themselves to be dragged down into hell while living in the richest nation in the world. And I am not talking about their wealth or the lack thereof.

For it is one thing to be poor, and it is another thing to be poor in spirit. Get your spirit right and you can walk with your head up with just a penny, while the man next to you with ten million in the bank has his head hung low and is thinking about suicide because he has a wife that does not love him and kids that hate him.

For man is evil by nature. This financial freedom gives us our personal independence from the Collective, from the Hive. It gives you freedom to send your children off to private schools or to home school them. My friend, you should thank God right now for your freedom.

"The presidency of the United States and the key cabinet departments of the federal government' were 'taken over by a private organization dedicated to the subordination of the domestic interests of the United States to the international interests of the multinational banks and corporations. This seizure of public power by private interests is the most serious political scandal in American history. Watergate was someone named Martinez breaking into the office of the Democratic National Committee in the dead of night.

Cartergate is David Rockefeller breaking into the Oval Office in broad daylight." Craig Karpel

David Rockefeller created the Trilateral Commission, a sister organization to the CFR. This allowed him to place key people into the Carter Administration. Nearly every major post in the Carter Administration was a CFR, Trilateralist or both.

This was the dark days of Betrayal and Deception for America. Bush 41st, Clinton 42nd, and George W. Bush 43rd are all members. The Brotherhood was now fully in control of America's highest office. It was one thing to back a player; it was another to get a Worship Master in plain view and in play. They could now influence the whole society.

"...the problems of governance in the United States today stems from an excess of democracy... Needed, instead, is a greater degree of moderation in democracy...Democracy is only one way of constituting authority, and it is not necessarily a universally applicable one. In many situations the claims of expertise, seniority, experience, and special talents may override the claims of democracy as a way of constituting authority." The Triangle Paper. 8, The Crisis of Democracy. Publication of the Trilateral Commission in 1975

Interlocking Realities

"The problem of concentration of economic wealth has been of concern to Congress and the public for many years. On occasion, this concern has led to the enactment of important legislation, particularly between 1890 and 1914, and again during the New Deal Era. Since World War II, the nature of the problem has changed considerably, in large part because of the dramatic growth of institutionally managed funds, including mutual funds, insurance funds, employee benefit funds, and private trust funds held by bank trust departments. It appears that the trend identified in the 1930's of major corporations in the United States being controlled by corporate management because of the wide dispersal of stock

ownership among large segments of the public, may now be giving way to a new trend towards control of these vital elements of our economy through control of the voting of large blocks of stock in these corporations held for beneficiaries by a relatively few giant financial institutions." (1968 House Subcommittee on Domestic Finance "Commercial Banks And Their Trust Activities: Emerging Influence On The American Economy.")

Their goal seems to be to have us so interlocked in all our affairs that we cannot move without their knowing. They control our banks, commerce, trusts, and health insurance. That way, we will have nowhere else to turn. It is already too late.

You may have never looked for them, but they are there. They are in the Bank where you deposit your money. They in the college that your son or daughter is attending, and they own it also. They own the Politician that you voted for.

They will soon own the public schools also, yes; they are getting ready to name schools after sponsor companies. Already they own the newspaper and the magazine that you read. You say, 'What do you mean?' What I mean is, there are less people in the world now with more control and power over what you and I hear. I mean think of a Wal-Mart giant newspaper company running mom and pops out of business. I mean think of a mom and pop radio station giant buying up all the local radio stations, that is what I mean.

When you have a giant, you can set your eyes on him and influence and control him easily that have thousands of independent vocals of dreams and hope. But we Americans like our freedom cheap and easy, like our oil. We had laws against that, but Reagan took care of that.

H.G. Wells

Born Herbert George, the fifth and last child to Sarah Neal and Joseph on 21 September 1866 in Bromley, Kent, this British writer was best known for his science fiction novels, The War of the Worlds, The Invisible Man, The Island of Doctor Moreau and The Time Machine.

He was a prolific writer, and an outspoken socialist, but an anti-Marxist. Most of his works contain some social or political remarks and comments. He was born into a lower middle class family.

Growing up, he tried many jobs he failed in. In 1883, he became an assistant teacher at Midhurst Grammar School; it later became the Royal College of Science. There he studied biology under T.H. Huxley, father of Aldous Huxley.

He entered the Debating Society of the School. He joined the Fabian Society, which he later left because they were not as radical as he wanted them to be. And he was one of the founders of the Science School Journal. It was during these years that he became interested in reforming society. Throughout his life, he sought better ways to organize society. He wrote many Utopian novels.

His ideal government was a World State, he considered this inevitable. He envisioned a planned society, with advance science, did away with nation-states, and awarded people by merit and not by birth, and this government must be a democracy.

But he came to believe that the average world citizen was ill-prepared to decide the important issues and the government would fail if it was a paramilitary democracy.

Wells believed in a society run by Elites, that is: scientists, organizers, engineers, and others with merit. But he would like to see the common man have as many rights as he could. He, like the others, set in mind the Global State that we would one day face. And the Elites in the world would be running it.

Wells wrote the books The Open Conspiracy: Blue Prints for a World Revolution in 1928 and The New World Order in 1940.

George Orwell

He was born Eric Arthur Blair on 25 June 1903. he was born in Motihar, Bengal in India. His father worked for the opium department of the Civil Service, it was a lower middle class family that he was born into. He attended St. Cyprian's School and then went on to Eton where he became a King's Scholar.

After these schools, he was not able to attend a university. Because of that, he joined the Indian Imperial Police in Burma. It is said that he disliked Imperialism and later resigned to become a writer.

He entered several menial jobs and traveled from country to country. In 1936, he went to Spain and to fight for the Republican side during that Civil War, this was against Francisco Franco's Nationalist uprising. By mere chance, he joined a militia for the Worker's Party of Marxist Unification, (POUM) rather than the communist International Brigade.

This was a revolutionary socialist party. But later after the suppression by the communist and his narrow escapes, he became an anti-Stalinist.

Orwell supported democratic socialism. He also supported a Federal Socialist Europe, which was outlined, in his 1947 essay "Toward European Unity". It is said that his political view shifted over time. But that he was always on the left side of politics.

Aldous Huxley

Was born on 26 July 1894 in Surrey, England to a well-established, prominent family in the English aristocracy. He went to Oxford and started his literary.

He wrote 47 novels, his personal best was Point Counter Point published in 1928, but his highest literary achievement came from his novel Brave New World, which was published in 1932. This was a book with visionary foresight that looked into the future and saw a spiritually deprived society in a one world technocratic state.

He moved to the United States in 1937 and moved to California. There, in search for deeper spiritual pursuits, he encountered eastern mysticism and explored psychedelics. He influenced groups like the Beatles and the Doors

He was fascinated with the ridged social structures he had seen in life. Many think of his books as warnings of a one world dictatorships, but they are more like the blueprints of various world councils, to set forth a true-life one world socialist government.

Huxley's work centered on the methods for keeping the mob or common people in a permanent state of child-likeness. Ever needing and wanting the state and its systems to take care of them. All the while keeping the mob in love with their enslavers. We have reached that state for some. Our only hope is in helping the individual, we have lost the nation.

Nine

United Religions

"No one will enter the New World Order unless he or she will make a pledge to worship Lucifer. No one will enter the New Age unless he will take a Luciferian Initiation."
David Spangler, Director of Planetary Initiative, United Nations

There is a move to unity. It has many names. Let us take a look at the URI or United Religions Initiative. This is a global Assembly; it serves as a partnership with the United Nations to bring together the world's Religious leaders.

Its first time summit was hosted by the UN to discuss and celebrate the global interfaith movement. It had much help with the likes of Mikhail Gorbachev's organization, The State of the World Forum.

This ensured the success of this event and others like it throughout the year. Among the participants was Pope Paul II. The purpose of the URI is to bring together all the world religions to form an organization.

This no doubt will lead to a global religion. Several of the URI's activities are directly supported or initiated by the Vatican. Millions around the world have signed the Initiative put forth by the URI charter. This gave birth to the United Religions Organization.

Christian Dominionism

On the rise in America, if not the Western world is a call for a Christian Theocracy or Theonomy. This idea comes from the

Dominion or Dominion Theology teachings on the rise in many churches in the USA, Canada and Europe.

As a trend of the new America, it has come at the right time, for this the age of Empire, and the fall of the American Republic.

This political-religious concept can be found in the Protestant, Evangelical and Fundamentalist camps. Their aim seems to be to seek political policies based on their religious beliefs. This in, and of itself is no surprise.

For we all remember the days of the Christian right in the 1990s. But this group seems to want to take this a step farther and subject the world to the rule of the Word of God as they interpret it.

Most Christians understand that God gave us responsibility over the earth. But there are those who believe that there must be a Western domination of the world and over everything in the world. They have found many causes to justify a Theocracy over all the earth, with America leading the way.

They feel that they must manifest the call by God to assume all authority upon the earth. From Genesis 1:26, to Matthew 28:18, to Genesis 1:28 right down to Romans 8:4.

They see God commanding them to exercise that authority in His name upon the earth. Their goal is to bring all things including societies and cultures into the subjection to their God.

Who are they?

They are men like Rousas John Rushdoony; to him the great commission is a mandate for action. He says,

"Be fruitful, and multiply, and replenish the earth, and subdue it: and have dominion over the fish of the sea, and over the fowl of the air, and over every living thing that moveth upon the earth." (The Institutes of Biblical Law. Pg 729)

"....Man is summoned to create the society God requires." (The Institutes of Biblical Law, pg. 3-4)

"The man who is being progressively sanctified will inescapably sanctify his home, school, politics, economics, science, and all things else by understanding and interpreting

all things in terms of the word of God and by bringing all things under the dominion of Christ the King." (Foreword to Greg Bahnsen's Theonomy in Christian Ethics, 3rd edition, xii)

Other leads for this movement are Francis A. Schaeffer. Works by Van Til are cited by those in this movement as inspiring. Now those outside of Christianity would like to lump all Christians together as radical, fundamentalist, bible-believing terrorists. Many hate Christians and Christianity and will use this to hurt the innocent Christians in America and the world.

And anyone that stands up for a cause will be labeled in the most negative way. But these groups and their beliefs fall right in the plans of those seeking a New World Order. Now we all should know that we do not need federally funded Christian charities; we do not need a state funded religion. But that is what this will bring.

The left and the right would like to set aside democracy to defeat the other by any means necessary. The culture and religious wars that are in the United States as well as in the Middle East are only going to heat up.

The True Nature of the Antichrist

"...I scoff at the notion that anyone other than a pope could be the antichrist." W.F. Strojie, conservation Roman Catholic scholar in, Last Days of the Catholic Church, 1978, p.3 (self published).

The Jesuits are good. They have turned and defeated Protestantism and placed it on its head. They have entered a Protestant country and subdued it by flare and cunning. Like Absalom, they have taken the kingdom right from under the eyes of the king. But unlike David, we have not discovered that we are dethroned.

They started by creating the myth that the Antichrist will be a secular monster. It is there in all the films and books that you read. This has been a windfall for Rome. Religious leaders around the world have joined in to blast the Antichrist, but in doing thus, they miss the HOLY FATHER. That way the Muslims, Jews, Roman Catholics, and Protestants can join in one voice to condemn this future secular monster.

But this belief is not from the Word of God, which teaches us of a false prophet, Antichrist and a Beast, and these three are one. It is this false religious leader that brings together all the false religions. This man is atheistically a Pope. But preaching that will not get you in fellowship with the ecumenical movement. The late Pope was a bridge builder; he reached out to any and all. It did not matter, he wanted fellowship with demons and angels, and he did not care. So it will be in the last and most powerful antichrist. Lenski, a conservative Lutheran scholar, wrote the following about the Antichrist:

"This is an apostasy. It is therefore, to be sought IN the church visible and not OUTSIDE of the church in the pagan world, in the general pagan moral decline, in Mohammedanism, in the French Revolution, in the rise and spread of Masonry, in Soviet Russia, or in lesser phenomena. We should not confuse the little antichrist with the great Antichrist, the antichrists OUTSIDE of the visible church with the great Antichrist INSIDE of it." (Emphasis his).

This will be (the) man of sin, the son of perdition, and the son of hell. He will be a deceived deceiver. He will be the false Christ, but the people will love him. This man will call himself a man of peace, and for a price, he will bring peace into the world, but the price will be your body and soul.

Pope John Paul II announced to the world that there are "many paths to God." We see that Catholicism, like Judaism, has slid further down in spiritism and paganism. For once, you leave Christ and His Word, you have left everything. As Jeroboam moved the people to worshipping a false god, so has the Vatican moved the world. Israel and Judea, there is nothing left for America and the world but judgment.

Ten

State of the World

"It's a great huge game of chess that's being played–all over the world-if this is the world, you know."
(Through the looking Glass-Lewis Carroll)

To see the direction that the World is going, we can keep our eyes on men like Gorbachev, Dalai Lama, Dr. Carroll Quigley and the David Rockefellers of the world. Gorbachev in his role as a spokesman for the New World Order has acted in conjunction with the UN and other World bodies. He has put forth his Earth Charter; in his own words, this is his "Magna Carta for Planet Earth". They will be the new "Ten Commandments" that will provide a guide for human behavior in the global community.

The UN Millennium Assembly and Summit provide solid new directions on implementation of global government. With the parallel People's Assembly (A People's World Parliament) which is being put forth as a permanent body of the U.N.

Enter the Society of Jesus

"It is a riddle wrapped in a mystery inside an enigma; but perhaps there is a key"-Winston Churchill

Churchill, I believe, said that of Russia, but it stands today as a broken nation. It will rise once more, just give it a chance. The nation within a nation is the Vatican and all its hidden power and forces. Let us take a look.

Certainly the most prestigious and powerful secret society of Roman Catholicism is the Jesuit Order. This is the CIA of the

Vatican. And the Jesuits Order along with Opus Dei runs the American CIA, which runs much of the American Intelligence community if not all after 9/11.

John Paul II has acknowledged his undisputed leadership of this Jesuits order. They have a special vow of obedience to the Pope of Rome. It implies the destruction and enslavement of the Protestant Christian and liberal minded Jew in America, then the world.

Stand or fall

"The Council on Foreign Relations is the American branch of a society which organized in England...believes national boundaries should be obliterated and one world rule established. The Trilateral Commission is international...is intended to be the vehicle for multinational consolidation of commercial and banking interests by seizing control of the political government of the United States. The Trilateral Commission represents a skillful, coordinated effort to size control and consolidate the four centers of power-political, monetary, intellectual and ecclesiastical." (With No Apologies by Senator Barry Goldwater)

Where do we fit in to all of this? What if we, as Americans, see things differently than those from the rest of the world? What if we do not go along with this World Order push? How will we be dealt with? Too late, we have already been dealt with, and we have surrendered. Do not worry, if you so much as think you are going to fight back, they will hit us with one of their dirty bombs.

You see, we have had our little national emergency, and out went The Constitution and The Bill of Rights. We were set up a long time ago, as we expressed our collective votes and elected voices in government. We push ourselves farther and farther away from God.

My friends, I ask you, how were we conquered, and who has enslaved us? Who has taken away our Freedoms of Speech, our

Freedom of the Press and our Right to Assembly? It was not the Iron Fist of the Russians, nor was it the weight of armed forces of the Colossal Chinese.

We have fallen victims to our own fears. From the words of Lincoln,..."**Shall we expect some transatlantic military giant, to step the Ocean and crush us at a blow? Never-All the armies of Europe, Asia and Africa combined, with all the treasures of the earth (our own excepted) in their military chest with a Bonaparte for a commander, could not by force, take a drink from the Ohio, or make a track on the Blue Ridge, in a trail of a thousand year.**" Abraham Lincoln in a speech in 1838.

It was our own lusts and fear. "**[T]he battle has moved to inside America...I tell you, freedom and human rights in America are doomed. The U.S. Government will lead the Americans people-and the West in general-into an unbearable hell and a choking life.**" BBC taped interview of Osama bin Laden after 09-11-2001.

We have sacrificed our freedom for a false security. We are moving toward a Police State. This has been designed by the American elite and the Global Elite. All power will be concentrated in Washington, and that power will be placed in the emerging World Government in New York, the United Nations.

Lincoln warned us, "At what point then is the approach of danger to be expected? I answer, if it ever reach us, it must spring up among us. It cannot come from abroad. If destruction be our lot, we must ourselves be the author and finisher. As a nation of freemen, we must live through all time, or die by suicide."

We have as a nation turned our backs on God and now we are reaping what we have sowed. Others will in turn enslave the players and actors within the government. No one will be safe.

Under the National Security framework they work and make their plans, none dare speak the truth or they would be found out and dealt with.

America has become unethical and immoral. Our movement bases their actions on lies and disinformation. This keeps their actions hidden under deep classification. This secrecy only fosters more secrecy. They have gained control.

They operate for their own purposes; see Swordfish and Enemy of the State. Some are just "Cowboys" operating outside of all laws and ethics; this is at any and all levels of government.

They are working on creating a global collapse of the U.S. economy. This will be far worse then what happened in the 1929 crash. Then will come Martial Law. We will be crying out for Martial Law, we will be begging them to restore Order as one city after another implodes.

Just as it was in New Orleans. No matter what law, no matter which liberty, just get it done, we will say. They have set it up just as they did in the 1920s. In the U.S. Economy, millions are invested, or shall I say gambling, in the money markets rackets on Wall Street. The little guy, who is not able and truly cannot afford to, is now taking chances at the Wall Street Roulette Wheel like never before.

Controllers of Knowledge

Not everyone in these groups whether in government or in private have the knowledge and understanding that they need to make a wise decision! There is no doubt in my mind that the majority of Americans that work in the U.S. government, at any level, from any branch of the Federal, State and Local level are not in the know. There are some yes, but not many.

In general, they are the best of people with only good intentions for their fellow Americans in their hearts; they have put their lives on the line to protect us daily.

For the most part, those that operate these positions in these organizations are not in the Conspiracy nor do they have any knowledge of it. They are very good people in each one of those factions or branches of government.

But the decay of America in its moral and ethical mindset, affects us all. When this nation's morals decay, we decay, if we do not take a mighty stand and resist the tide of spiritual pollution. We should see this in the action of our troops and ourselves.

Who is guilty?

We all are if we look closely enough. We do not need a conspiracy to sin. We do not need total government to abuse our authority, with family, friends. You can read about it in every major newspaper in any part of the country, generally every day.

We all have sinned and come short of the glory of God. We are a bunch of angels. Americans will not own up to it, but we are the biggest hypocrites there are.

That is the problem with a future socialist humanist government. It is one thing to know you are evil and to fight against it, it is another to think you are holy unto yourself, a god. Needing no redemption, needing no savoir. That is what we will have soon.

Just look around, just watch the news, people have already used their power without and within the Conspiracy to turn these agencies in to tribal gangs. And the more power we give them, the more power they will use against us. In the end, they too will fall into the same trap as the rest of us, and be enslaved.

The same fate will come upon the local Police Officer, the Sailor, Soldier, Airman, National Guardsmen and the Reserves Member. They will be used to enslave us and in the process, will be enslaved. For when we take away the rights of the Common Man, we take away the Rights of us all.

This move to slavery cannot be helped and it cannot be stopped, it is the will of God. The United States has to pay for its sins. I just do not know when. It truly is useless to fight against it. Your only hope is to get your own spiritual house, your own soul in order. As when Christ told His Disciples that the destruction was coming and to be prepared to leave or die within the city. You must decide now.

You can be like the Jews when told by Jeremiah that the Judgment was coming and to prepare to be ruled, or resisted and died. This New Order that is now coming will be far worse, maybe not in the beginning but certainly in the End.

Conspiracy: "An agreement, manifesting itself in words or deeds, by which two or more persons confederate to do an unlawful act, or to use unlawful means to do an act which is unlawful."

Eleven

Self –Extermination:

"My own doubts came when DDT was introduced. In Guyana, within two years, it had almost eliminated malaria. So my chief quarrel with DDT, in hindsight, is that it has greatly added to the population problem."
Alexander King, president of the Club of Rome

We are our own greatest enemy. Mankind will kill itself off. Let us now take a look at Margaret Sanger. Let us see what spirit she was guided by. She was an open supporter of the Nazi plan for genetic engineering of the German population. I wonder what would have happened if Hitler had cloning back then, where would we be now? She was for the propagation of a "super race". She was a believer in the necessity of the extermination of 'human weeds'.

She believed in the cessation of charity, the segregation of morons, misfits, the maladjusted and the sterilization of the 'genetically inferior races'. To get all this going, she helped found Planned Parenthood. She would be proud how they have continued on with her legacy. I know that they are truly proud of their past, I can tell by the way they have continued on the road to elimination of the "human weeds" and "the cleansing of society."

Only God knows the secrets that lie within the hearts of men. Throughout this book, I have tried to place before you the evidence of their hidden desires, to make known their hopes, and their views with their own words and public deeds.

It is up to you to judge, may the Lord open your hearts and eyes. In her magazine "The Birth Control Review", Margaret

Sanger supported the "Infanticide program" promoted by Nazi Germany.

Her personal fight, her Crusade, I should say, was to save the planet from such as mentioned above, especially the Negroes, for that she formed her "Negro project". That is why you will find these death houses in the big inner cities conveniently placed in the poorer and more ethnic neighborhoods.

The Environmental Wars

"The evidence of global warming keeps piling up, month after month, week after week. How long is it going take before those people in Congress get the message? People are sweltering out there...The future holds significantly higher temperatures still unless we do something about it." Vice President Al Gore

"The five warmest years recorded since the 1400s all occurred in the 1990s." President Clinton

"As the early readings necessarily predate the European discovery of the Western Hemisphere (1492), Australia (1606), New Zealand (1642), please make it clear whether the temperatures recorded by the Aztecs, Incas, Australian aborigines, and Maoris are in centigrade or Fahrenheit or whatever." Mathematical Statistician, J. Gart

Wicca

An (if) it harm none, do what thou wilt

This is know as the craft of the wise. The handy work of occultism and the works of Aleister Crowley can be seen in this new religion of today, Wiccans deny it. In any case, it is a patchwork of beliefs. What I see is an old mystery religion, an evil with a new face; this is one of the new named religions for our new age. It has within it several degrees.

This new religion is nothing more than replacing an old book cover, but keeping the same old contents with the same old story. This Pagan religion is found in many countries the world over.

It is referred to now as the Old Religion. It took its rise in 1954 when a British civil servant came out of the closet after the British repealed the Witchcraft Act. He started what is now referred to as the Gardnerian Wicca, there is also Alexandrian Wicca. Most traditions of Wicca are still secretive and require an initiation ritual.

Now here is the good part, Wicca is a religion, and those that belong to it are witches. But they will tell you that their beliefs are not necessarily witchcraft. Ok, got that, good. Now let us move on.

Now they can and do worship different things. Some worship a goddess, others a god. They observe festivals of Sabbats, and full moon Esbats.

Now they say they are distinct from witchcraft because witchcraft does not imply any specific religion, ritual elements, and ethics. And witchcraft is practiced in various forms by many different religions and by atheists.

I would say that they have organized witchcraft into a higher (lower) order or form. But that it is still witchcraft, they have just decided to try and do away the stigma associated with witchcraft. And they have blinded many people into believing their lie, and it is a golden lie.

Now let us look at the art. It has rituals that involve casting spells, divinations. They claim to limit their purposes to good only; white witch hmm? So what is it, a religion with witchcraft in it or witchcraft? A little evil can go a long ways.

Their gods and their Symbols

Now let us look at their gods. We have the goddess, Gaea or Mother Earth and her lover the Horned god; they are equal in most groups, in other groups they are not. Their names may vary from group to group also. But the spirit behind the cult stays the same. Some are polytheist, animists, or pantheists. Their symbol is the circumscribed pentagram.

Loners and Groupies

Now there are solitary or eclectic Wiccans and they are non-initiatory Wiccans. They can work alone or in causal groups rather than organized covens, hives or groves. The ones that join covens typically seek an ideal number, reported is 13.

It takes about a year for the initiate in a coven to study in the group before their full initiation takes place. Within these groups, they are at times promoted to higher ranks.

False Hope

This came from our dear President: "I don't think witchcraft is a religion. I would hope the military officials would take a second look at the decision thy made."

A Conservative Christian named James Clement Taylor had this to say about the false persecution of the Wiccans. It truly is a sad day for Christianity when its sons and daughters are blind to what is the truth, he states: "these people of Wicca have been terribly slandered by us. They have lost jobs, and homes, and places of business because we have assured others that they worship Satan, which they do not. We have persecuted them…" Now let us take a look and see a rose under any other names, is it still a rose?

The Sacred Groves

"The groves is the centre of their whole religion" Tacitus

In the times of the ancient Pagans, the groves were a place of worship to their gods. And so it is today, with the Witches and Wiccans and Pagans on the rise, so are the groves. The rise of the false religions only speak to the day in which we live in. They will increase, while we must decrease.

The American Elite have their own grove; it is called the Bohemian Grove. There they have a two-week getaway. Only male members of our society are allowed. It is said to be a time of male bonding. There they play out human sacrifices effigy. Every American Republican president since Coolidge has taken part.

The atmosphere is said to be occultic and Masonic in organ. The center of their worship is a 40-foot stone owl. The voice of the owl is Walter Cronkite. Druidic rituals are performed by members wearing priest-like costumes of red, black and silver robes. This act of human sacrifice is called "Cremation of Care or Dull Care"

There are over 2,700 members or guests, with a waiting list of 10-15 years long.

The State Powers

Telecommunication Act of 1996

Freedom from Religious Persecution Act-HR 1685

International Religious Freedom Act of 1998-HR 2431

"Our task of creating a socialist America can only succeed when those who would resist have been totally disarmed." Sara Brady, Chairman, handgun Control, to Senator Howard Metzanbaum, The National Educator, January 1994, Page 3.

The growing involvement of the Vatican and its allies in global politics and world religions prepares it to take its long awaited and prophesied stand on the world stage.

Alice Bailey is known as the 'mother' of the New Age movement. She is also known as a promoter of the Catholic Church, she said, The New Age would, "rest upon the foundation of a newly interpreted and enlightened Christianity...being universal in nature." And no major distinctions exist, "between the One Universal Church (Catholicism), the sacred inner Lodge of all true Masons, and the innermost circles of the esoteric societies."

(Source-The New World Religion-Part XI-Identifying the New Order by Gary Kah)

We should be able to see the shape of things to come in her statements. These words also tell us of the deeds to come. They tell us of the influence and power of her movement. They tell us of the alignment of the Roman Church with other groups like hers.

They show us that this growing global rebellion against God is on the move. And with its new position and power, it will set its occult mandates over the people and over the will of God. Just as it has set man-made doctrines over the Word of God.

They show us how they envision a religion that will be promoted and enforced though these world systems of churches, lodges and covens. The Ecumenical Movement has bridged the gap between Christianity and pantheism.

Now the Pope will hold in his hands once again both the Temporal and the Ecclesiastical powers of the world. The world will then truly be a Holy Roman Empire. And an Empire has to have a Dictator.

The UN will stand as his earthly power and the Vatican as his heavenly power. He will be the knot that holds the world together, that is until God moves. Like Daniel and the three Hebrew boys, you will bow or you will burn and if you bow, you will surely burn.

The dye is cast on the path to a Religious Police State. It lies in the many laws and Bills that have come from the Illuminati controlled government in Washington D.C. We have HR 1685, The Freedom from Religious Persecution Act of 1997 sponsored by Virginia's Rep. Frank Wolf and Sen. Arlen Specter of Pennsylvania. This is the same Arlen Specter of the single bullet theory on the assassination of JFK. This is the making of a tribunal to go along with the office Of Religious Persecution Monitoring in the White House.

The director answers only to the President. He is charged with reporting on abuses against religious minorities. Serious abuses would trigger automatic economic sanctions (buying and selling). This was being set up to monitor religions and to track individuals.

This bill would have created a Cabinet level agency whose mandate would be to provide surveillance over religious groups. But it failed, but in its wake came HR 2431 International Religious Freedom Act of 1998, which was signed, into law (Public Law No.: 105-292) by President Clinton on Oct. 27, 1998.

This moved the Office of Religious Persecution Monitoring from the White House to the State Department, giving the Secretary of State new powers of overseeing religious discrimination and in reporting its finding.

It also appears to delineate these activities to foreign countries. However, it also permits the President to waive any sanction for governments when it serves U.S. national interests. President Clinton then issued an Executive Order that federal jobs must guarantee workers religious freedom on the job. Therefore, they must have some way of monitoring them in the work place. (Source-Jeremiah Project)

And to ensure that we are never told the truth, the whole truth and nothing but the truth, our elected leaders in Congress pass the Telecommunication Act of 1996. This act allowed the mega mergers of media conglomerates to become ultra monster mergers. As a result, today, a handful of multinationals control most of what is said in the U.S. about our military, financial and Political system and their actions both at home and abroad. General Electric is in the weapons business and in the news business, a blatant conflict of interest. They have cut off most all avenues of escape. And the war of ideas is only getting started. (Source- http://www.alter.org/story.html?StoryID=14873)

"The spiritual Hierarchy (demonic realm) of the planet, the ability of mankind to contact its Members and to work in cooperation with Them, and the existence of the greater Hierarchy of spiritual energies of which our tiny planetary sphere is a part-these are the three truths upon which the coming world may be based.

...The New religion will be one of Invocation and Evocation, of bringing together great spiritual (occult) energies and then stepping them down for the benefiting and stimulation of the masses. The work of the new religion will be distribution of spiritual energy."

"The new religion must be based upon those truths which have stood the test of the ages...they are steady taking shape in human thinking, and for them the United Nations fights." (Alice Bailey as quote by Gary Kah in The New World Religion-Part XI Identifying the New Order)

Twelve

Patriots and Soldiers

Democracy: "A government of the masses. Authority derived through mass meeting or any other form of direct expression. Results in mobocracy. Attitude toward property is communistic... negating property rights. Attitudes toward law is that the will of the majority shall regulate, whether it is based upon deliberation or governed by passion, prejudice, and impulse, without restraints or regard to consequences. Results is demagoguism, license, agitation, discontent, [chaos}." -U.S. Army Training Manual No. 2000-

There are 2 out of 5 Gulf War I vets on disability. There are 209,000 VA claims, with 161,000 getting payments. Americans were told that the casualty of this quick victory was only 148 killed and 467 wounds in the Gulf War. This out of the approximately 540,000 vets that served in and around the war zone.

But the truth of the matter is that nearly two of every five are on disability as a result of illnesses they sustained during that conflict. 5,000 veterans are plaintiffs in a lawsuit that accused companies of helping Iraqi President Saddam Hussein build his chemical warfare arsenal.

They are among tens of thousands who came down with Gulf War Syndrome, a debilitating series of ailments that can include chronic fatigue, skin rashes, muscle joint pain, memory loss and brain damage. They had fought overseas for their country and they had to fight for their lives once they returned home. (Source WorldNetDaily)

The Workers

Americans, I feel, fell for the propaganda concerning the North American Free Trade Agreement (NAFTA) because of greed, we wanted it all. But what it was a continuation of the "Bretton Woods" agreement, in 1944, at the Bretton Woods, New Hampshire meeting of some 40 nations.

Several proposals came forward and several agreements were made. These agreements set the groundwork for the United Nations, General Agreement on Tariffs and Trade (GATT) and other global structures to take away our rights as a nation.

Slowly, they have been pushing forward more and more global structures to limit each individual country's ability to run their Foreign Trade; they must do so inside these global power structures. These pacts further promote our relinquishing our sovereignty and our responsibility over our own national economy. We are in a controlled meltdown of our physical-economic systems.

We no longer act as a nation acts on its own, for our own national interest, whether foreign or domestic. The mutual interests of these trading partners, who are non-government cartel companies, control us. We are back to the British East India Company, which invokes "Rule of Law" that bounds us to enforcing their trade agreements.

In Seattle, Washington, they were scheduled to hold their third ministerial level conference of the World Trade Organization, where their goal was to commit to a new "Millennium Round" of talks to continue to liberalize world trade, with negotiations running from the year 2000 to 2003 or beyond. Representatives from around the world were present, a reported 50,000, from 134 nations.

The Imperial Legions

The Multinational Non-Democratic Institutions were the outcome of deregulation. Now with the mega companies dominating every economic sector, from medicines, to livestock feed, to gasoline, to telecommunications, to food and water. We are now set up for a global controlled society. Or a global controlled Famine.

With the power and reach of the WTO, these mega companies and their polices impact all aspects of society on the planet. These rules are written by and for corporations with inside access to the negotiations, all information or impute by citizens are ignored and denied and the proceedings are held in secret. Now these companies control the food supply, for example in the US, the U.S. based Cargill, Inc. acquisition of Continental's grain division, now constitutes an operation controlling 60% of U.S. grain export stocks, the largest in the world. U.S. based Archer Daniels Midlands (ADM) is the largest soybean processor in the world. U.S. based Smithfield Foods; the largest pork processor accounts for 20% of the pork produced in the United States and produces more than 20% of the hogs slaughtered.

Governments cannot take actions against a mega company, for the behaviors of these mega companies are protected by the WTO, which has ruled that it is illegal for a government to ban a product based on the way it is produced. So, child slavery in China continues by the power of the WTO. Source (http://www.nex.net.au/user/reidgck/WTODEP.HTM).

The Mafia

The Cosa Nostra, which stands for our thing or this thing, is ours. Is a true secret society. It came about in the mid 19th century on Sicily. It served as protection for the estate owner and then moved to the politicians and gained much power. Now there was a Brotherhood in Italy going back to the time of Cesar. And many Italians had flooded the area.

Today, we cannot only talk about the Italian Mafia any more. We now have the Mexican, Russian, Irish, Japanese Yakuza, Chinese Triads, Albanian, Cuban, Black, Indian, Jewish and many other groups that make up crime families and organizations the world over.

Now the Mafia in America and Italy has connections or shall we say, has a relationship with the Catholic Church. The Mafia is still said to be the most powerful crime organization in America. It still controls organized crime in Chicago and New York.

They were not seen as criminals at first, it seems, but as heroes and tough guys that were there for your protection. In the 1860s, Law Enforcement was not there for the poor and weak Sicilians. The Mafioso were said to stand for pride, noble, honor and all that was right.

The Adoption Ritual

This is an orientation ritual for the Neophyte. He is brought before an older member of the family by at least two or three "men of honor" from the family he is to join. One of his fingers is pricked and his blood is spilled onto an image of a saint, referred to as a sacred image.

This image is then placed into the hand of the Neophyte or initiate and lit on fire. He must then stand the pain of the burning; passing the image from one hand to the other while it is consumed by the fire.

During this time, he is professing or swearing to keep with the principles of the "Cosa Nostra" and swearing that may his flesh burn as did the image of the saint if he fails to keep his oath.

The U.S. and the Mafia Alliance

The American government has used the Mafia on several occasions. During World War II in the invasion of Italy and Sicily, operational military intelligence was obtained from American crime bosses being held in U.S. jails.

In his book The Catanese, author Alfio Caruso states that the U.S. Office of the Strategic Services allowed the mafia to recover during the war and that this allowed for their 60-year reign of power after the war.

Some kind of Alliance can be seen. In Operation Gladio, many groups that were anti-communist were used as "stay behind" paramilitary forces sponsored by the CIA and NATO to counter communist influences in Italy and in other western European countries. This operation reached as far as Uruguay, Brazil and Argentina just to name a few.

Gladio's existence was later acknowledged by the head of the Italian government on October 24, 1990, Prime Minister Giulio Andreotti. This operation linked together neo-fascists, mafia, Propaganda Due, a Masonic lodge also known as P2, and the strategia della tensione or strategy of tension.

P2

Now let us take a look at the Italian Freemason Lodge, Propaganda Due or P2. This lodge was founded in 1877; its real power and influencing years were from 1965 to 1981. This lodge was said to be organized for visiting members. In the mid 1960s, it is said that this lodge only had 14 permanent members. But in the coming years, its power would reach into major banks like Banco Ambrosiano and the Vatican Bank, and with its link to Operation Gladio, its reach would be global.

This lodge was used by the prominent and elite to penetrate the Italian government, and other governments and the press, this was done to prepare them, to form a resistance movement just for the threat of the Communist winning over the Italian government during an election.

The action that was taken by this Lodge and its members were as bad, if not worse than what they feared the Communist would do. Great sums of money were being moved around the world for both legal and illegal operations.

Heads of state were being assassinated as members of the lodge stood by and watched. It was their duty to investigate and make arrests, this did not happen. One of the murdered was Prime Minster Aldo Moro. He was killed by the Red Brigades because the Italian Security Services refused to deal with his abductors. Another one to be assassinated was the Prime Minister of Sweden, Olof Palme in 1986.

P2 funds were allegedly used in the Iran-Contra affair and the S & L sandal. The source for this information came from Richard Brenneke and Ibrahim Razin, both claimed to be former CIA agents. Their story was told to Ennio Remondino a RAI journalist. As their story unfolds, we see a tale of drug trafficking, illegal arms trafficking and government destabilizing operations.

Now the lodge had rapidly expanded under the leadership of the Worshipful Master-Licio Gelli, its membership reached 1000 members within a year of his rise to power and under his guidance. Many of his new members worked in civil service jobs for the Italian government, at that time Italian civil servants were mostly forbidden to join secret societies. Then in 1976, the year before total darkness hit the earth, the Masonic authorities are said to have withdrawn the lodge's charter.

It was or still is an illegal secret shadowy government that was run from an illegal Masonic lodge, it was discovered in Italy, in 1981. This Lodge's purpose was to be ready to take over the Italian government, if the communist won the election.

It has been linked to Operation Gladio. The Vatican Bank helped funnel covert money to the Solidarnosc in Poland and to the Contras in this operation. We find this information in Operation Gladio in Wikipedia, which quotes several sources to include an article by the Observer in November 18, 1990, as reported by Statewatch. The report states that there were declassified secret service papers that revealed the link between this Secret Order and illegal American operations in Europe.

It names key officials to include, Henry Kissinger, Ted Shackleton, deputy chief of the CIA in Rome, its Grand Master Licio Gelli, head of the neo-fascist P2 lodge, General Alexander Haig, then chief of staff for Nixon, he later became Supreme Commander of NATO and Secretary of State.

P2 members included Italian Businessmen, bankers, diplomats, Cabinet members, intelligence chiefs, and members of parliament, military leaders and others.

Like Phillip Dru, the Worshipful Master had a War Plan. It was called the Democratic Rebirth Plan; this was a declaration of the lodge's intent if the action had to be taken. Gelli's goal would be to form a new government with the political and economic elites. They would lead Italy into a more authoritarian form of democracy.

Thirteen

The New Dark Ages

We have on the horizon a New Age-Dark Lord; he will be Master of The Alliance between the Trade Federation (NAFTA, EU, G-7, G-8, G-10, and G-24), the Intergalactic Bankers and Commerce Clan (Business).

How will you and I fit into their plans? As Hollywood gears up for the War on Terror, it is prepared to conduct a fully fledged Propaganda operation for the Department of Defense.

This is what appears to have happened in the Kosovo War also. For the Cable News Network (CNN) and National Public Radio (NPR) have acknowledged that eight members of the US Army 4th Psychological Operations (PSYOPS) Group served as interns in their news divisions and other areas during the Kosovo war.

A total of five PSYOPS sergeants were assigned to the network's Atlanta headquarters. These included two at the Southeast bureau, two at CNN Radio and one at the satellite department. They also worked at the Washington DC headquarters of NPR.

They worked periods ranging from six weeks to four months from September 1998 through May 1999 on such programs as All Things Considered and Morning Edition. This was reported in the World Socialist Web Site, the French publication Intelligence Newsletter, and emperors-clothes.com on CounterPunch. Yes, I sometimes go to the enemy and different sites to run down the truth. I have learned, if you want to know the hidden truth about someone or something, go and ask his or her enemies, they can spin the truth, but they will give you leads that the friends will not.

The story goes that Colonel Christopher St. John, Commander of PSYOPS, who commands 1, 200 soldiers and officers stationed at Ft. Bragg, North Carolina, was reported to have said as reported by the Intelligence Newsletter that the cooperation between the army and CNN was a textbook example of the kind of ties the US Army wants with the American media.

Rather than outright military censorship as was done in the Gulf War, NATO tried to use more subtle means to regulate the flow of information while suppressing unfavorable information. Rear Admiral Thomas Steffens of the US Special Operations Command (SOCOM) said at the symposium that the military should have the capacity to gain control over commercial news satellites to bring an "information cone of silence" over areas where Special operations are taking place.

But it does not stop there, we see Walt Disney World hiring former employees from the Central Intelligence Agency for their theme parks. What are we seeing taking place, are their plans coming into plain view, the move from entertainment and News into total mind control in the market place? Just a question.

Compare

Do movies have meaning; can they convey a hidden message? Of course, most fairytales of the past carried moral messages. Essayists like Huxley, Wells and Orwell convey their socialist ideas in books, essays, and now movies. Now our own generations of propagandist are hard at work.

They are very subtle, and they sometimes use double speak. That gives them plausible deniability! So let us take a look at the Masters of story-telling of our day.

We have Gene Rodenberry with his Star Trek series and its United Federal of Planets. And its socialist elitist views. We have Steven Spielberg and E.T. here we have the master of the alien invasion with Close Encounters of the Third Kind and Taken. This has acclimated the people to believe a lie.

And third we have the Star Wars Trilogy of George Lucas has momentary replaced our myths and our legends with his own? Why? To expresses his mythological views of life and to show his deeper psychological motives of how he conducts his life.

These films have been a hit the world over. And they are laying a quiet groundwork for the New Age believers. They are placing in the mind of the viewer a seed to be used later.

In this myth, George Lucas has outlined for us a Tyrannical Emperor, the Pope, who works from behind the scene to subdue through lies and deception all free nations. He uses the last superpower with the latest technology to transform the world into the image that he desires.

This servant lord is a member of a secret society, he works from within the system to betray it; he takes the Republic and turns it into an Empire (George Bush 43rd).

As Hitler did, this Emperor uses his people well. The Dark Lord uses celibate Warrior Monks to infiltrate any all nations. He places one side against the other, causing wars and confusion to cover his own actions. Knights of Templar vs. Knights Malta, USA vs. Russia. SS vs. SB.

With a heavy hand and new laws, this Dark Lord, this Vicar, attempts to extinguish the young Rebellion that is formed against him. He is able to do this through his much-trusted slave, Darth Vader (George Bush/Loyola). "W" will go to no end to serve his evil master. He betrays his own, crosses over and receives the power from the Dark Side. He travels the World putting down any and all resistance to his master, and calls all small and great to bow down.

We see Obi-Wan Kenobi sacrificed himself for the good of the Force and become an ascended master, a New Age Master. He is now able to return in a spirit form and Channel his thoughts into the young Skywalker.

The Force is an entity, which is not personal, nor is it intelligent. But can be used by the good and the bad. Thus, we see the practice of White and Black Magic before our Eyes. Not knowing that this Magic is all evil.

Sound likes what is happening today in your newspaper, for we see the Senate taken over by a Dictator (George Bush) as he uses the threat of War. Like Hitler, he pledges to return his power to the Republic once Order is restored. But now we are told that this war will last for a 100 years. Therefore, we must wait a hundred years for Liberty and Freedom! (What Star Wars Teaches Us by Michelle Kinnucan Published on Friday, May 10, 2002 by CommonDreams.org, http://www.blazing-trails.com/jesmith/ar/starrek.php3?)

Wars for your Sons and Daughters

There is more than effort information out there to show operation after operation of the U.S. government through the CIA dumping drugs into American cities for blacks, hippies, and poor whites.

We can truly see that with Rock and Roll, which is a powerful force for subverting cultural, social, political normalcy and morals and has brought on a negative change wherever it has traveled. It has been used by the devil to destroy the minds and the body of the young generation.

Every 40 years is a new generation. This is a post Rock era generation. This second generation is set up to fall by its own hands. But they will make good soldiers or "cannon fodder" for the NWO.

In his book Tomorrow's Soldier, David Alexander speaks of the NWO thinkers and indirectly brings out their plans of operations worldwide. He speaks of OOTW and MOBA: Operations Other Than War and Military Operations in Built-up Areas. We see the plans they have, the ones they allow us to see, and the technology that is emerging and has emerged.

We see the fears of wars and future battle zones that they have planned for themselves and us, but they feel that they will be protected. We see that they are preaching of the total war, where every one is a combatant, therefore at risk and needing their protection. We see the making of the Universal Soldier or world soldier.

They talk of regional and big power confrontations. Now from the past, we know that there has always been a local, regional, or a world order. And in the course of time, there would arise an individual or a group, which would desire the wealth or property of another. For the most part, these conflicts are and were handled on a city-by-city, country-by-country, region-by-region, or nation- state basis. This order or world condition has at times been in a flux as in the Twenty-Century's Two World Wars. Which were actually two European Civil Wars, which America allowed the Globalist to pull us into?

Going back to the Tower of Babel, we see the seat of a regional order not to the degree or scale that we now see ghastly approaching us today. But they had at that time a common language, as we do with English, and meeting place, as we do with the U.N. They had a large regional government and a popular Dictator in Nimrod. The people love a strong ruler, even when he rules wrong. They had Nimrod, we have Bush. And we have those that lead him.

"At times, we must be willing to subordinate our national objectives to the greater objectives of the networked nations and multinational firms with whom we interact." Lieutenant Colonel William R. Fast United States Army (BALANCING ENDS, WAYS AND MEANS IN THE INFORMATION AGE)

We have seen Pagan Rome die and be replaced by Papal Rome. And it is on the rise once again as a mighty empire of a warrior priest. We have seen the League of Nations die and the hope of peace in the First World War. Only to see it rise again like a Phoenix from the ashes after World War Two as the United Nations. Out went that Old World Order.

Now the stated goal is to persuade countries to resolve their differences without resorting to violence and to establish an economic and social agenda. Sounds nice on the ear and looks good on paper. But it means death to billions, for it is peace by slavery.

They know to carry out this mandate; they must expand into every sphere of our everyday life. Therefore, they have erected special bodies such as UNDP, UNICEF or UNCTAD, to touch every soul on this planet. With the United Nations Charter 99, a charter for global democracy, world rule is set forth.

To do this they have targeted the sovereignty of nation-states as an expendable and outdated concept. Agents of the Globalist or the Hive have grown in power in America starting as far back as Jimmy Carter. Bill Clinton was their most-outspoken agent. He and others like him have preached that we must come to rely on their ideas of a holistic codependence, that the individual must submit himself to the dictates of the elite; they have claimed this special preeminence for themselves.

And now Bush Jr. calls us to his amoral ethics, as he abandons the Founding Fathers and betrays our Western Civilization in order to purge the world of those who oppose his view of World Domination, both foreign and domestic. In addition, he calls us to be accountable to him and to the elite members of his Administration and to use only their model on what it is to truly be an American. So I ask you, what kind of American are you?

"Those who excel in war first cultivate their own humanity and justice and maintain their laws and institution. By these means they will make their government invisible"-Sun Tzu

The term we hear today, The New World Order, has been around for quite sometime. To achieve this latest World Order or Global government, the Elite classes of the world, either Religious or Political, are now in the process of eliminating the Old World Order. What is the Old World Order; it is the system of government known as the Nation-State. As we have seen the

States in America lose their rights to govern, so will America in this Global Nation lose its rights.

They are fostering a super-capitalist and Socialist government like the ones we see in China, Russia and the EU. They envision as a first step a regional and then a global government to replace the Sovereignty and independence of each nation-state. This is being done through NATO and the EU expanding. The United States of America itself will certainly cease to exist in the form of government that our Founding Fathers intended. The U.S. Constitution and The Bill of Rights will have no power and no meaning to the people in this new global community.

With the renovation and strengthening of the United Nations and its agencies of education, nutrition, health care, population, immigration, communication, transportation, commerce, agriculture, finance, and the environment to name a few. It will reach into our every day life and it will cover every aspect of existence.

We will soon see the accomplished formation of a world government, complete with its own army, world parliament, and world court and revenue service for global taxation. This is the way we are heading, the question is will it be achieved in the next one to five years, or the next ten years to twenty? Our God only knows.

But day by day, their plans are coming into plain view..."We are not going to achieve a new world order without paying for it in blood as well as in words and money." Arthur Schlesinger, Jr., in Foreign Affairs (July/August 1995).

When asked in 1954 by Norman Dodd, an investigator for Congressman Reece's Committee, what their objective was H. Rowan Gaither, President of the Ford Foundation said, "We operate here under directives which emulate from the White House... The substance of the directives under which we operate is that we shall use our grant making power to alter life in the United States such that we can comfortably be merged with the Soviet Union." Also, he said, "[The task is to] covertly lower the standard of living, the whole social structure, of America so that we can be merged with all other nations." You tell me, have they succeeded? We are our industries, where have our farms gone, overseas, the same place our taxes dollars went to finance our own downfall.

Dialectic Process

I hope that you are growing in knowledge of the staged arrangement and the plots. I hope that you can see more clearly the groups and players on the stage. I hope that you can also see our place in this grand chess game and see our role in this major theatrical production. For the US comes in as the Thesis, then Russia enters from the side as the as the Antithesis, now this presents the free world with a problem, therefore The UN as the Synthesis becomes the global solution. We grew tired of that game so they gave us invisible men to fight; therefore, we have impossible odds in this improbable war.

Ok you say, when did all this get started and where did they come from. Let us take a look at the leadership that flowed into America and helped to create it in 1776. What were their outlooks and what were their motives. And how were they influenced and by whom.

Even if they were true to heart, they needed money, they had to be somewhat controlled by the International Bankers. Someone was paying for the flow of imports and exports and the other needs of the Colonies. Then came the thinkers and idealist of 1846-1848. And there arose the ideals of Communism in Europe.

As time went on, we see American and European dollars keeping the Russians afloat. Then in a deal that does not make much sense, we see Presidents Franklin Roosevelt and then President Truman give Eastern Europe to the Russians. We see the hand print of the 'silent' Elite establishing their three dimensional chessboard so that they can play. Now we have the terrorists to take the place of Russia, they still need to keep us in fear, so we can be ruled much easier.

Our Manufactured Foes

As more and more Americans are brainwashed by the Evil-vision, we see the groundwork being laid for a Global Defense Force against an Alien Invasion. When we were but a young empire, we had many challenges and true foes, this rallied the nation behind its leaders. But now since we are the greatest Empire upon the planet, the only foe seems to be the Judeo-Christian faith and the Constitutional guaranteed rights and Freedoms by and for the people.

Enter the space aliens, they are bound to replace the earthly and mortal foes- the terrorists. For once, we have subdued the nations and placed the Republic safe and sound into a Police state. Once we have set up our 10 kingdoms or spheres, or regional Empires. Even though they will only last for a short season. We will need a greater fear for the people, a greater call to arms, and a greater reason to maintain the order and keep the working masses entertained and occupied. The Industrial/Military/Intelligence/Luciferian Collective or Hive must be maintained at all cost.

One person working tirelessly to bring these facts and technologies into the open is Dr. Stephen Greer of the Disclosure Project. I believe I heard him on the Art Bell radio show as he blamed the "narrow minded" (Author's words) Christians of holding back man on his quest for higher technology.

You see, we are in the way. They want to kill the barking dog that is trying to tell them there is a robber at the door. But they refuse to listen. He is calling for congressional hearings into the issues of UFOs and the free energy technology that he and others believe were reverse engineered from this alien race or something.

Then you have the Donald M. Wares of the world who are all ready to up-link and be plugged into the alien psychic. But he is right about this planet being set up to form a New World Order. And in my opinion, men like him are preparing the minds of the people for that Order. He is preaching nothing less than complete mind control. It seems to me that he is a voice for some group or group within a group, and is informing us on how they have waited until the "right" general/leader came along, one without Christ, drugged, entertained, and ready for full deception.

They have waited for over forty years for this Christian Nation to die out and be replaced by those who know not God. But a small group still remains and they have to be removed or dealt with or both.

The brain of the Hive lies within the Vatican. But the front organizations are the Bilderberg Group, CFR, the Masons, the Ford Foundation and the Trilateral Commission. And its front men and their support families, the Henry Kissinger, the Rockefellers, the Rothschilds, the Dulles, and the Bushes to name a few make up some of their financial and Political venue. Like the Black Pope in the Vatican, you may know of him, but you will never see his hands as he moves the pieces on the 3-Dimensional chessboard from behind the smoke screen of lies and false doors.

They rely on the ultimate in the thesis-antithesis-synthesis to manipulate the leaders and people of the world. They will succeed for they have the money to purchase and the technology to perform it.

We will soon witness the appearance of Extraterrestrials. It may be played out as a Space Alien War visited upon earth, with the Grays as the good guys and the Blacks, of course as the bad guys. With the Grays sharing with us their advance and now more than ever, vital weapons and humanitarian technology.

Humankind would completely and fully surrender its liberty and freedom to the Global Government with Emergency Powers. At once, the people would have a new friend to love and a new and fearful enemy to hate. At this time, a reported 80 % of Americans believe in Aliens aircraft, or UFOs.

They, the Elite, continue to generate crisis after crisis to bring on more laws and a tighter hold upon the American people. And it is truly working. From Y2K, to the Health Crisis, to the Ecological Crisis, Crisis of Family Values, Crisis in Education, Hate crimes Crisis and a pediatric disease Crisis. Big Brother is stepping up to the plate, to take your hands off the wheels of life, so that he can truly guide this spaceship Earth.

The next moves

Now they asked and answered this question long ago. How do we get to where we want to go from here? After they thought it out, they set into play forces that would take us there.

They know that they could rely upon the winds of change to blow our way. They also knew that they could create the small fires that would generate the winds, and from these small fires, they would fan the flames until they turned into a firestorm. And from these firestorms would come the lift that we needed. They would provide the direction that we would go.

Here, we see the wind beneath our global wings. They select a local conflict, say Yugoslavia. This little war allowed us to flex our European regional muscle. We were able to play in Russia's own back yard. It allowed us to reach out and steal someone away from their country and try them in the World Court. The world stood with us on that.

Then came Afghanistan, that government at first sought peace with us, but we needed war. They were destroying too much of the opium crops. That had to be stopped and we wanted a gas pipeline through the country. So war came, even as we let the terrorists fly out of the country and into safety.

Next came Venezuela, America preaches democracy, but only when it furthered our cause. We helped the Shah to power in Iran over an elected popular official. Now in South America we were willing to turn a blind eye to the rise of a Junta, all to secure the oil.

In Colombia, our ongoing dope trade has empowered us to stay in the area and operate at will. In Iraq, we saw an opportunity to secure a vast oil reserve, and with the coming peak in oil, we knew that it was time to move. The Elite knows that he who controls the oil wells controls the future.

And then there is Israel, or shall I say Jerusalem. This is the greatest prize of three religions. There is nothing man can do to stop the coming war. They will only delay it. So we know that they will try and that they will have a small peace, but for only a short time.

In the War against the breakaway republics, our NATO/EU/UN forces moved into the Caspian Sea area. According to a June 23 (2001?) story on UPI, the US trade and Development Agency announced on June 2, the US had awarded a $588,000 to Bulgaria to carry out a feasibility study for an oil pipeline.

Under this proposal, Caspian oil would be shipped by tanker from the black Sea ports in former Soviet Georgia and then pumped by overland pipeline across Bulgaria, Macedonia and Albania.

These huge oil reserves under the Caspian Sea have been a coveted prize for years. The Third Reich waged the bloodiest battle ever fought there, the siege at Stalingrad, in an attempt to gain control over access routes to these oil reserves during World War II. (Source: Jeremiah Project)

In our Global War on Terror, we see the foremost role of certain oilmen in Washington forming alliances with enemies of democratically elected governments, their goal is to foster in a government that is more agreeable according to their oil enriching plans.

In Unocal, we see former US government officials making efforts to launch several oil pipeline projects. Henry Kissinger, the former US Secretary of State, attended the 1995 meeting at which the first attempt at the trans-Afghan pipeline was announced. We see a paid adviser, Zalmay Khalilzad, an Afghan émigré who was later chosen by President Bush Jr. for the National Security Council, specializing in Central Asian affairs.

This ex-Unocal man was then made the special US envoy to his native country. He supervised the political affairs of the US selected Afghan leader on his day-to-day activities- Hamid Karzai, the interim president of Afghanistan, who also was a paid consultant for the oil industry, I believe it was Unocal also, before the war and was trained in America.

Now under the Karzai-Khalilzad-Unocal regime in Afghanistan, the pipeline plans have been taken off the shelf. On March 7, 2002, Karzai flew to Ashkabat, the capital of Turkmenistan, for talks with President for life Saparmurat Niyazov. On May 30, 2002, Karzai, Niyazov and Pakistan President Musharraf met in Islamabad to sign a memorandum of understanding on a gas pipeline project, beginning with a feasibility study.

The pipeline would run 1,460 kilometers from Turkmenistan's Dauleatbad gas field to Gwadar, a port in Pakistan on the Arabian Sea, where natural gas would be liquefied for export. The Asian Development Bank began studying routes for a shorter gas line that would bring Turkmen gas to Kabul and several Afghan mining sites. The $2.2 billion price tag for the trans-Afghan pipeline was far larger than the total amount of foreign aid pledged to the Karzai government and more than 10 percent of Afghanistan's gross domestic product.

"The real rulers in Washington are invisible, and exercise power from behind the scenes" Supreme Court Justice Felix Frankfurter, 1952

With the stationing of American troops throughout the oil-rich Central Asia region, the move was made to attack Iraq, the world's second largest oil reserve nation. The US led forces, which set to oust Iraqi President Saddam Hussein, opened up a bonanza for the American oil companies long banished from Iraq. This would dash oil deals between Baghdad, Russia, France and other countries and would reorganize global oil markets. Afghanistan was only a stepping-stone towards the overthrow of Saddam Hussein and the seizure of Iraq's oil resources.

Attacks had been launched in Yemen at Terrorists leaders also. The first major moves of the Global Elite were to bring the civilized world to the throat of the Arabs to subdue them. The new millennium world was made to fear Terrorism by Islamic Fundamentals as the old world was made to fear the ghost of the Communists.

We have learned how, at the height of the Cold War, US officers were given identification cards that named them as members of the Soviet Army. This status allowed them to roam through East Germany and overtly spy, take photos of naval vessels, installations, troop movement, radar antennas, and anything of interest to U.S. intelligence analysts.

This was a Secret Protocol, rarely mentioned in the histories of post-World War II Germany that allowed Soviet, U.S., French, and British officers to keep track of their opponents' activities in East and West Germany.

So we see in 9-11 that this act of betrayal was used to put Americans in their place, and before the world, the Arabs were made to fear the Atomic might of the Western world.

The American Globalist knew that by allowing an attack on American soil to take place, the American people would gladly surrender their rights and their freedoms.

The US then intensified its pressure on Saudi Arabia, the world's largest oil exporter, why? Some in the Bush II administration began hinting that the Saudis, along with Iran would be a future target after the conquest of the Iraqis.

A link to the Saudis and the so-called terrorists Khalid al-Mihdhar and Nawaf al-Hazmi, who were believed to have received help from Omar al-Bayoumi and Osama Basnan.

The FBI was said to have uncovered financial records showing payments from a Washington bank account held in the name of Princes Haifa Al-Faisal, wife of the Saudi ambassador to the United States and daughter of the late King Faisal.

Still reaching farther into the pie, the US backed an attempted coup in Venezuela, and then stepped up military intervention in Colombia. The two are the most important South American suppliers of oil to the US market.

This shows us the framework of the overall American policy of seeking to dominate the market in one of the world's most important and strategic resources, *oil*.

But the overall or the main action for Israel in this play will end in Israel. There will come a seven-year peace treaty with Israel. They will bring slavery to us in the name of peace. This consolidation will come soon after these wars have ended.

This is the West's New Crusade, as proclaimed by President Bush II, and all Crusades end up in Jerusalem. This one, I believe, will not be any different.

Global Union

Betrayal: "Is to be delivered, or exposed to an Enemy, by treachery or disloyalty."

"The developing coherence of Asian regional thinking is reflected in a disposition to consider problems and loyalties in regional terms, and to evolve regional approaches to development needs and to the evolution of a new world order."-Richard Nixon, in Foreign Affairs October 1967

The New World System

In the year of our Lord, Nineteen Fifty-Nine, the Christian Church in the United States made a terrible mistake. It tuned down the Voice of God going through the land at that time, and it was a final and fatal move by America. Now we see the majority of the people of this nation and this world going about their daily life completely ignorant to what is going on around them and what is to come to this generation or the next generation to come.

They seem blinded to the great social and political changes that are taking place, the move of the world power-Elite, world leaders and our own government are making terrible mistakes.

But why, because in 1954, God began to judge this nation and this land, that year the people of this Nation turned down the move of God that was taking place right before their eyes. But even then, God gave them a space and time to repent, but they would not. That opened a door for Satan to move in, and he has.

From Skull and Bones to Harry Potter, this nation is taken over by Witchcraft and Luciferian worship; there is no turning back. We have been controlled for a long time. "Fifty men have run America, and that's a high figure." Joseph Kennedy, father of JFK, July 26th, New York Times. There is statement after statement, or are you really listening?

The way things are

The world Elite see Global Democratization and Capitalist-Socialism as the system to bring the world together. This they feel will bring about the much sought after world peace, this utopia that so many in the world feels that they need.

America is the Vatican's Muscle for shaping the New World Order. The Vatican is the dominant force behind the UN. The road to the global government is paved through Rome. The Pope of Rome daily gives his views and recommendations on world troubles to the world leaders, and they are listening, even if they make a public display as if they are not.

He has hosted several meetings of political and religious leaders. He has sought the consensus of world leaders on many of his plans and ideas. He is seeking and getting a religious unity of the people of the world, to foster a political one. He has laid the groundwork though his personal work and though his many ambassadors.

His muscle: The US armed forces, the many police operations since Vietnam has turned our military into a global police force, walking a planetary beat. With the development of new weapons systems, i.e. infrasonics, nerve agents, and low energy lasers, we have enhanced, not lessened our commitment to ruling the world and lying to the folks back home.

The Council of 13, the Council of 39, the Council of 300 and the Council 3,000. These are the high Councils of wise men that rule the world. The Illuminati, are they for real? Or are we chasing after a ghost? They are for real and they are very clever; many have searched the world over to find them. I believe the truly enlightened ones reside within the walls of the Vatican.

No other capital in the World has the Vatican's far-reaching power. No other nation-state can have an army of willing servants within every country and every government in the world, including Iraq, with its 1 million Christians, and still be seen as a friend. And if the rumors are true, what Mr. Malachi Martin brought out in several of his books, the Vatican has turned to unadulterated worship of Lucifer.

Then truly, we see a shift in their Leadership. Then we must acknowledge and prepare for the appearance of the Anti-Christ, for it is later than we think. For the whore has fully sunken into sin.

These men, the players, the movers and the shakers of this movement, of this cause, are not fully aware of what their action will do to this nation and to this world. They seem blinded also to where they are headed and do not seem to realize how their actions will bring about the enslavement to the world community and to themselves.

From Churches around the world, from their priest and their preachers, we hear a call for a revival that will never come, especially to this people and to this nation. For the people of this nation have left God, and God has left them.

I am not against any person or people of any religion, but I am against the religious and political systems that have enslaved and destroyed men's lives and souls.

The vast majority of Christians and Romans that worship every Saturday or Sunday do not know that God has left their Churches and their nation, because it was no longer His church, but a social club, a dance hall or a fashion show. God calls us to, "...Come out of her, my people, that ye be not partakers of her sins, and that ye receive not of her plagues. For her sins have reached unto heaven, and God hath remembered her iniquities." REVELATION 18:4-5

Betrayal of the Church and Betrayal by the Church!

"If you know the enemy and know yourself, you need not fear the results of a hundred battles. If you know yourself but not the enemy, for every victory gained you will also suffer a defeat. If you know neither the enemy nor yourself, you will succumb in every battle." –Sun Tzu

Cassandra was one of the daughters of King Priam of Troy. Legend says she was given the gift and power of prophecy by Apollo, but was then doomed to be disbelieved by others because she refused him her love. So too, it seems, are the words of the men of God of today.

For their words are doomed to fall on deaf ears, just because they refuse to conform to the love of this world. And like Troy, those who refuse to hear them, seek to imprison those that would call sin, sin.

The world tries to silence the only ones that can sound the warning when God's judgment is near. I started writing this book back in 1990 during the First Gulf War, I have had many setbacks, but I pressed on. I wanted to share with the reader my views of the coming years and the troubles ahead.

In the upcoming novel that I am writing which is called The Fading Republic, you will see my view on events to come. The scenarios, the conversations of the characters are mine. The use of my literary license can be seen. But we all know that something is coming, we all know that, but the how and when it will take place is up to God and God alone.

The only escape is being in the presence of God's mercy, through His Son, the Lord Christ Jesus.

That Truth is found in His Word. This upcoming book is dedicated to all those who have served this once great land and nation, while they served their God. Anyone can serve a country, but to serve the living God as you do so, that is the challenge. May God's blessings and mercy smile upon you, and make your hearts open to His true Revelations of His Holy Word and of His "Message of the Hour".

Disclaimer

I would like to say first, that this is not a book about hate. It is a book about True Love. The kind of love that gives you the courage to tell a friend, your boss, a lover, that they are wrong.

This love makes you willing to endure the pain; even if that means that, you will lose that friend or that job. You are willing to do this in the right season and in the right spirit, even though it hurts you to have to be the one to carry them the bad news. So here, I am anyway, the bearer of bad news. We shall see what lies in store for me later.

Some will say that this book is a form of hate literature and hate speech. But then they said the same of the words of Christ. For He dared to tell them that they were in error, and that they were wrong. I have to bear my cross, and with His spirit, I know I will hurt many that I love.

But in the end, if they can receive the light of this book or one like it, then it will be worth it all. On the other hand, if not one soul finds my words enlightening, and rejects them out right, I will still have fulfilled my duty and my calling.

I would like to say now that I do not hold any malice or dislike for any of the people, organizations, or groups mentioned in a negative way in this book. I am not condemning anyone for their alliances, allegiances or memberships that they hold.

This is a book about spiritual good and spiritual evil. It is about spiritual being, being manifested upon the earth through the human agents of God or Satan. As Christians, our fight is with Satan and his spirits, in high places and not with man. God bless you as you read, may your eyes be opened.

In Summary

I hope that you have came away with more knowledge and understanding of the world and the groups and major players in those groups than you had when you first arrived. If not, you were one of the few that have taken the time or had the opportunity to have someone bring this to your attention in the past. Either way, you were blessed.

I hope that I have given you some issues for you to think about concerning the New World Order. I hope that you can see that if one joins the Mafia, the Illuminati, the Jesuits, or the Masons, they all take similar initiation rights and steps to become a fully fledged member. That is the key to my thought in writing this book.

I hope I have connected the dots for you so that you can see a parallel in those groups and their masters behind the scene. I would like to thank you for taking the time and reading this book and its material. May God bless you in a special way!

THIRTEEN

Our Fading Republic

Our world, our republic is changing and has changed over the centuries. Have we fully come to terms with our own approach to the world, to this modern age? Can we get an understanding of the intellectual mindsets of the past ages and its people? Can we catch their influence on our beliefs and on our mode of thinking? Maybe, let us take a look at what has been told to us and what has been suppressed. Let us now take a look and see what we can find.

A Perfect World

In a perfect world, they will need a perfect man. This man has been sought out throughout the ages. Each Age has sought out the 'modern man'. He has been educated and cultured, but still he is a lost and dangerous soul.

All of the great men and women of the past have tried to reach this idea in by one way or another. But in this day and in this age, we have tried something that no one else has ever tried before, Genetics. With our modern science how close to God, will we get? How close will God let us get before He stops us?

We are not unlike the Greeks, the Romans, the Germans, the Soviets, and the Chinese before us. We have learned to nurture and to use nature to try to create the perfect man. Yet, he is still a failure. But why?

We have grown and matured as a culture and we have tried to elimate the true God from our lives, we have taken Him out of our educational system, from our Churches, from our schools and from our homes. Mankind has done this to remove the old superstitions of the past, but all we have done is to replace them with the new superstitions of today.

Modern man has a new god-Lucifer. You see, this modern society has, as a whole, set up idols of comfort and glory and has forsaken our Lord Jesus Christ. This Age, this Laodicean Church Age, has deceived it own self.

Now we see the move of the 'low culture', this Hollywood culture from the movies, from the music, from Rock and Roll, from Hip Hop. With its ungodly dressing styles, portrayed by biker gangs, the religious pagans, now, even the educated savages have taken to dressing up as modern day Pirates and Thugs.

Where has this new modern lifestyle invaded, the middle class in America! Now this style is on display to the world. This is what they see.

This lifestyle, this low moral lifestyle and not the Christian's positive role model. This is what we have projected to the world. This undressed lifestyle, this sinful beggar lifestyle; this is our image and gift to the world.

But you say, why does it matter? It matters because what was once was considered a failure is now considered a "Modern Marriage" or a "Modern Lifestyle".

America fails to see that our modern world is nothing but a broken world. With broken lives all around us. Nevertheless, there are more freedoms and rights in this Nation-State World Order than our forefathers had. We are truly blessed. And this blessing has be come a curse around our neck. We will answer to God for it.

We have lost our courage to say no to sin and sinfulness. Therefore, we will fall back into slavery and into a world more dreadful than our forefathers ever knew.

Where did all this come from? Some would have you believe, that this evil sprang from the Black Ghettos. Others would have you believe that it comes from the White Slums, but I say it comes from Hollywood, Madison Avenue, and from MTV.

But they can only put out what we allow them to, therefore it comes from us. When "modern man" ran God out of his home, his church and his school, there was a void to be filled, and now it has been filled. And it is filled with filth and evil.

Who could have done this? Ask yourself, who has the resources that could influence the middleclass in American in such a great way? Who has the planes and the boats to bring in the drugs, at time with the permission of the America government? Who controls what is on the, that Evil-vision, which sits in your home influencing your thoughts and views of the world. Look around you and tell me who would have, who could have done this?

Do you think that the poor and the needy of America had the money and the power to start this Billion-dollar Drug Trade? No, they use the drugs; they use the guns, and the filth of the world. But those with the money and those with the power, they are the only ones that are able to bring in the illegal products or the special merchandise into this country and make a profit. More than just oilmen come from Texas and Arkansas. More than Wall Street Tycoons live in New York City.

Look around you; do the research, which group or groups in the past fought to keep you from having a translated bible in your hands? Which group or groups fought to remove religion and its barriers from your life and school, which groups sought to breach the morals of the American people? And they have. Who wanted this? Look around you, do the research and then tell me.

The Tares Reign Supreme

We now see those that once were the outcast of any decent society rise up and take power and authority in America. And with this rise, they bring with them their character and their sinful practices.

This is what America has come to, a pool of the most unrepentant, perverted. A nest of liars, cheaters, thieves, fornicators, and adulterers. They are now our leaders and our children's heroes. Millions bow down to them, millions worship at their throne of popularity.

And to speak against them, is now a Hate crime, and to think that their actions are unholy and unwholesome is to think evil against them, and that is a Thought Crime, "Mens Rea- a guilty mind". We are ripe now for the taking. The Sleeper has awakened! But have you?

Right wing vs. Left wing

As a nation, we are divided. And as a divided nation, we cannot stand, we will fall. The Global Elites has conquered us; we are set to fulfill the plans of the International players. In fallen for their lies. They have placed us in the Blue state or the Red state; they have us thinking that this is a fight with the left or the right. It is not.

But, many people are being misled into the two camps set up in America, if not the world. I guess we all like things simple and easy, but this fight is not simple nor is it going to be easy.

Whether you are a conservative or liberal, you are, being misled into believing your way is right. And by believing this you. You are more than willing to align yourself with any person, or group that is an enemy of your enemy.

Consider please, that each path has lead us to a bigger government, both ways are leading us to dissolve our borders and to rush into regionalism with Canada and Mexico; both parties, both ways are leading us to a capitalistic-socialist Global Nation. But Why?

Now in both parties we can see their errors, some are easily defined. They are on the extreme, whether it is on the left or right. But in today's world, things are beginning to get blurred.

There is a merging of ideas and idealisms. Take for instance, capitalist-socialism. This seems to fulfill both dreams of the differing parties. This idea also seems to fit into the financial and economical void that will be left after the ouster of America on the world stage.

This Global Nation that is being born will be fostered and driven by consumerism, it will be a money driven society, but unlike America, it will be without the freedoms and the rights of the people. Let us now take a look at some major Globalist. President Clinton, the liberal, brought us NAFTA, why? It was against the workers of America and the American Unions. Who put him up to this?

Next came President Bush, he entered the world stage as a conservative, right? But he brought America big government and less liberty, why?

Who could have put him up to that? And what of his power base and his backers? The moves of both men was against what their parties and their supporters believed. This was against their political platforms. Why?

If they left their foundation of power, who did they believe would support them? They seemed to have no fear of losing the support of their base, but why?

We are in the days of the crossing over. You see for the Democrats, they could not say no to Clinton, if Clinton lost, they lose their prestige. And for the Republicans, they could not say no to President Bush. So they were used to accomplish the opposite of their platforms and of their beliefs.

It would seem hard to believe until you read their origins and their backgrounds. There you will find that in the secret and powerful organizations of the world government, they were reborn.

You say this capital-socialism will never work. Well, let us look at China; this is our little experiment on display to the world. It seems to be working well enough for them, right?

Now you can keep your head in the sand, as you keep on thinking that your party is representing you, but be warned, it is not. It has a higher calling and it is answering that call every day. Keep reading if you dare.

The New Country

We are on our journey to this New Country, this new world, which is being created for us, and we will arrive there soon. Most of us do not know that there is a world being created for us. And it is being created in the image of its builders! We are too busy, we are much too busy.

Now to find out where we are going, we must first retrace the steps that have brought us to this junction, how did we get to this place in the road thus far? Let us go behind the stage and peer into the story behind the story, and see what is really going on in this ever-changing world.

What has transpired on the back stage, far from our view within the New World Order? Let us look at the parallels that appear to connect the major groups and their players on the world stage. Who are they and where are they taking us? Please come join me on this journey of enlightenment.

My Goal

My goal has been to lay before you a global perspective of the New Order to come. To do that, I have brought before you many concepts. Some were new to you, others were not. In this book, I wanted to display to you the concept of the New World Order in a different way. I wanted you to be able to see the groups and players in their true light. I wanted to us approach this from a scientific, philosophical, and even at times a, humorous angle.

Knowing that people are political, social, rationalizing and spiritual beings. And what they contemplate and have faith in are among the most important things we can know about them.

So from knowing this, I tried give you a look into their hearts. To see their ideas about their God, or gods. Knowing this would l tell us a lot about them. That allowed us to look into their ideas about this present world order, and about the future social and political world order that they are trying to create.

As we take a look at e individuals and the groups that, they belong to. We were able to take a look at their views, their dogmas and their doctrines. An as we looked at the individual(s) and their heroes that they look up to and the groups that they have placed their loyalty with. We were able to take note of what these groups are seeking, their mission and their statements, we were able to see a part of the players and operatives that they may not have wanted us to see.

We can see that they are all men. They are the Elites among the Elite. They are writers and thinkers, so we looked into their writings and their spoken words, we were able to see their own personal nature and their personal beliefs come forth. We were able to see how their views and their ideas shaped them, and how they intend on shaping us and the world around us.

THE END

References

The New World Order by Pat Robertson ISBN 0-8499-0915-5

Lucifer's Great Plan-Conspiracy Theory? By William E. Blase.
http://www.zianet.com/wblase/endtime/conspira.htm

The New World Religion/Engaging Evangelicals Newsletters by Gary Kah
http://www.cowan70.freeserve.co.uk/new_world_order/trilater_commission.html

The Dewitt Tabernacle C/O C.W. Wood

Jack Newell and Devvy Kidd ("Why A Bankrupt America?")

Project Liberty, P.O. Box 741075, Arvada, CO 80006-9075

http://en.wikipedia.org/wiki/Mafia

http://en.wikipedia.org/wiki/operation_Gladio

http://www.stragi.it/index.php?=vicenda&par=p2

http://www.skepticfiles.org/socialis/cosiga4a.htm

http://en.wikipedia.org/wiki/Wicca

http://www.wicca.com/celtic/wicca/christian.htm

The World's Mastermind: by Adrian Salbuchi

Jerry Smith Newsletter

Jeremiah Project

http://www.mt.net/-watcher/nwofamousquotes.html

Christian News, 1993 by Michael A. Hoffman

Researcher, Vol. 4, No. 3; 4/93, Flashpoint

http://www.jesus-is-lord.com/anti7 & anti8.htm)

http://www.threeworldwars.com/albert-pike.htm

http://www.weirdnessandstrife.com/knowledge/bio/pythagoras.html

http://en.wikipedia.org/wiki/Pythagoras

http://en.wikipedia.org/wiki/Gieuseppe_Mazzini

http://www.biblebelievers.org.au/protocol.htm

Cephas Ministries

http://www.thebereancall.org/Newsletter/html/1990/sep90.php

The Order; Anthony Sutton

http://en.wikipedia.org/wiki/Fabian_Society

http://en.wikipedia.org/wiki/H._G._Wells

http://en.wikipedia.org/wiki/George_Orwell

http://www.conspiracyarchive.com/NewAge/Huxley.htm

http://en.wikipedia.org/wiki/Peak_oil

http://en.wikipedia.org/wiki/Project_for_the_New_American_Century

http://en.wikipedia.org/wiki/Club_of_Rome

http://www.clubofrome.org/organisation/index.php

http://en.wikipedia.org/wiki/Neo-malthusianism

http://en.wikipedia.org/wiki/Malthusianism

http://en.wikipedia.org/wiki/biderberg_Group

Adrian Desmond and James Moore, Darwin ISBN 0-7181-3430-0

http://en.wikipedia.org/wiki/Elitism

http://en.wikipedia.org.wiki/Elite

http://en.wikipedia.org/wiki/Globalization

http://en.wikipedia.org/wiki/Crusades

http://en.wikipedia.org/wiki/Spanish_Inquisition

http://www.informationclearinggouse.info/artice11238.htm

http://www.newyorker.com/printables/fact/050214fa_fact6

http://www.aclu.org

http://www.tomdispatch.com/index.mhtml?pid=1984

http://www.druidry.org/modules.php?op=modload&name=PagEd&f

http://www.rotten.com/liberty/conspracy/bohemian-grove/

http://en.wikipedia.org/wiki/Dominionism